Obscurity to Success
in the Oil Business

Obscurity to Success in the Oil Business

Discovery of Parshall Oil Field in North Dakota

Michael S. Johnson

MICHAEL@JOHNSONGEO.COM

OBSCURITY TO SUCCESS IN THE OIL BUSINESS
Discovery of Parshall Oil Field in North Dakota
Published by Karras Publishing
Denver, Colorado
Copyright ©2016 Michael S. Johnson. All rights reserved.

No part of this book may be reproduced in any form or by any mechanical means, including information storage and retrieval systems without permission in writing from the publisher/author, except by a reviewer who may quote passages in a review.

All images, logos, quotes, and trademarks included in this book are subject to use according to trademark and copyright laws of the United States of America.

Library of Congress Control Number: 2016941660
Johnson, Michael S., Author

OBSCURITY TO SUCCESS IN THE OIL BUSINESS
Discovery of Parshall Oil Field in North Dakota
Michael S. Johnson

ISBN: 978-0-9975086-1-1

BIOGRAPHY & AUTOBIOGRAPHY / Personal Memoirs
BUSINESS & ECONOMICS / Industries / Natural Resource Extraction

QUANTITY PURCHASES: Schools, companies, professional groups, clubs, and other organizations may qualify for special terms when ordering quantities of this title. For information, email michael@johnsongeo.com.

All rights reserved by Michael S. Johnson and Karras Publishing
This book is printed in the United States of America.

KARRAS KP PUBLISHING

To Kay, lovable and elegant,
my closest companion for fifty-seven years

Cover photograph: © Vern Whitten Photography

An Oasis pad in Parshall Field (30-T158N-R92W), site of eight horizontal wells with simultaneous frack job being performed (forefront). Dirt roads, cultivated fields and lined mud pits showing environmentally sensitive operations, which demonstrate compatibility of land use and oil exploration.

(Data courtesy of Oasis Petroleum Inc.)

Contents

Preface	xi
Family: Origins And Early Years	1
College and Career: The Early Years	17
Career Firsts: As a Petroleum Geologist	31
The Army: A Career Detour at a Historic Moment	37
Career Crossroads… and the Road Taken	51
Major Milestones: Amerada in Wyoming	59
New Partnerships: Personal and Professional	65
Apache: Joining a New Breed of Oil Company	71
Launching a Consulting Career	77
The Geologic Study Group	81
Wessely-Headington Years: Exploration Success	85
Family Life in Denver	91
Foreign Adventures and Intrigues	97
Our Family Blossoms	113
The Church: A Major Commitment in Philanthropy	123
An Interlude with the Russians	129
A Further Introduction to Oil Deposits	133

Oil-Gas Price History and United States Energy Policy	141
Future Energy Use: Importance of Fossil Fuels	151
Late Twentieth-Century Issues: Climate Change and World Events	157
Family Life: A New Stage Unfolds	161
North Dakota: Early Energy Powerhouse	165
Parshall Field: A Career Turning-Point	169
The Geologic Idea	201
Career Achievements Rewarded	205
Postscript	219
Notes	221

Illustrations

Plate I.	Alberta map showing location of Athabasca oil sands	135
II.	Mining operations, Athabasca	136
III.	Oil recovery from vertical well	139
IV.	Oil recovery from horizontal well	139
V.	Bakken wells drilled until 2006	196
VI.	Parshall Field 2016	197
VII.	Parshall Field-Current Size: 6 million acres	199
Figure 1.	Energy usage by type: 2015 vs. 2040	152
2.	Aerial photograph, northwest North Dakota	180
3.	The Yellowstone Lineament	181
4.	Schematic of how seismic data is produced, recorded and displayed	224
5.	Schematic showing seismic data over an anticline	225
6.	Schematic showing seismic data over a reef	226

PREFACE

U.S. oil exploration activity broke all records in 2015, triggering a much-needed increase in domestic oil production—only to be followed later that year by the collapse of oil prices and the subsequent slump in oil activity. Amid this dramatic, evolving landscape in the oil industry, I thought it important and appropriate to tell the story of the discovery of Parshall Field in North Dakota, one of North America's largest oil fields.

Before beginning, however, I want to acknowledge my debt to friends and colleagues who furthered my achievements with their support and advice. Four turning points in my career, coupled with some perseverance and tenacity, brought me a measure of success. I thank everyone for their contributions.

By the early 1980s, published reports confirmed that the Bakken Shale contained hundreds of billions of barrels of oil in place. The search was on. By 1989 Marathon had drilled the last of five Bakken wells in the Parshall area. By 1991 a few more Bakken wells were drilled by others. Small oil recoveries were made on tests, and non-commercial volumes of Bakken oil were produced. Horizontal drilling attempts had failed.

The Parshall area lay dormant for twelve years. No wells had been drilled and all leases had expired. In 2001 some 110 miles westward, the first successful horizontally-drilled Bakken field was being developed. In 2003 it was my idea to lease lands in the Parshall area. Later, with the help of Henry Gordon and a silent partner, about 44,000 acres were leased for only one to ten dollars per acre. EOG Resources subleased our acreage block and, using later-developed horizontal-drilling technology, drilled the Parshall discovery well. The field now covers more than six million acres, with estimated oil reserves in excess of fifteen billion barrels.

In this book Parshall Field refers to the entire Bakken oil accumulation in northwestern North Dakota.

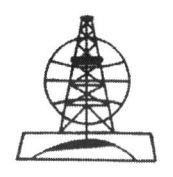

FAMILY
Origins And Early Years

In 1880, Greece was a rural, impoverished country. It was a critical time in the history of modern Greece. Only fifty-five years earlier, it had won its independence and freedom from Turkey—a struggle that ended four and a half centuries of slavery, pillage and looting that had kept Greece stagnant. There was no industry, and poor soil and mountainous terrain limited the farming of crops. Grapes, Greece's main potential export, could not find a market. The country had no raw materials or mineral wealth and needed modern roads and communications. Corruption and thievery were prevalent. Under these conditions, the people led a miserable existence. Dotting the hillsides were the numerous graves of all those who died from malnutrition, polluted water, and lack of medical care, including many infants and children. For all these reasons, an exodus began. From 1880 to 1890, a few thousand Greek emigrants started finding their way to America. The numbers would increase so that by 1920, about 185,000 had migrated—ten percent of the population of the free part of Greece.

It was during this troubled time that my father was born and raised in Kandela, a small village twenty-eight miles northeast of Tripoli, the largest city in Peloponnesos, the peninsula that makes up Greece's southern mainland (named after Pelops, the founder of the Olympic Games). His family lived in a two-room shack. Beneath the family's quarters were the chickens and sheep that—along with olive trees and dandelion greens growing alongside major springs—provided their main food staples.

My father's upscale residence in Kandela, 1905.

In 1896, at the age of only fourteen, sponsored by friends in Council Bluffs, Iowa, Efstathios Giannakopoulos left his family and friends and, with other Greek emigrants, landed in New York; a poor, uneducated boy looking for something better than the poverty, hunger, and isolation he had endured in Greece. The Industrial Revolution had begun, and America's economy was expanding rapidly, creating a demand for cheap, foreign labor. Immigrants were arriving in overcrowded ships suffering from bad food and sanitary conditions but enduring these hardships in exchange for eagerly sought after American jobs. Additional hardships awaited them once they arrived; immigrants were labeled as inferiors: unskilled and unable to contribute positively to society. Plus at Ellis Island there was an obstacle that every immigrant faced and dreaded, the Immigration Service. Everyone was compelled to pass physical examinations, primarily designed to identify immigrants with tuberculosis and other infectious diseases; those unfortunates would be sent back to their countries of origin. Immigrants were also questioned about their financial status and whether they had U.S. relatives or friends who could help them financially. Exploitation of young boys by padrone bosses was prevalent and is one of the darkest pages in the history of Hellenism in America. The idea that the streets in America were paved with gold was soon forgotten. My father was fortunate because he found his way to Council Bluffs, Iowa (a small town across the Missouri River from Omaha, Nebraska), where he had friends and sponsors.

His next twenty years are obscured by time. Handicapped by being an immigrant and unskilled in English, he found work doing odd jobs along with his Greek friends, primarily in the Council Bluffs and Omaha area.

Because it was a main station of the Union Pacific Railroad, Omaha became a center for Greek immigrants. The railroad itself offered jobs and was also the means of transporting cattle to a growing meat-packing industry. By 1910, hundreds of Greek immigrants lived in the Council Bluffs-Omaha area, employed mainly by the railroad, meat-packing, and related industries.

By 1920, he had become conversant in English and achieved a measure of financial stability. He had started to live the American Dream and applied for his U.S. citizenship. Becoming a naturalized citizen erased his status as an alien and filled him with pride.

On arrival in America, immigrants took any jobs they could find, but my father did not want to spend his lifetime working for others. Recognizing the opportunity offered by a growing, thriving country, and defying his language difficulties, he and many of his countrymen ventured into businesses of their own. He moved to Maryville, a small town in northwestern Missouri, and opened a sweets store with his nephew as his partner. This was his first venture into entrepreneurship.

My handsome father at age 29.

In 1921, using his naturalization document as a passport, he returned to Kandela to marry my mother, Vasiliki Pappathanasopoulou. The marriage was arranged by the two sets of parents. My mother was betrothed to my father before she even met him. At that time, Greek parents arranging a marriage were primarily concerned that the bridegroom was not a drunkard or gambler and was a good provider. The bride needed to be pure of heart (and everything else); good looks and personality were secondary. Romance would come later. Years ago, I noticed that in their wedding picture they are neither smiling nor holding hands. When my father first left to come to

America, Vasiliki had not even been born. He was now thirty-nine years old, fifteen years older than his bride.

Many years later, my mother would tell me that he came into their marriage with assets of sixteen thousand dollars—a huge sum then, equal to $175,000 in today's economy—accumulated over his many years of work. She was from a large, prominent village family. Her father was the village priest, the last of a long line of Greek Orthodox clergy. My mother was the eldest of eleven children, of whom only five would survive childhood. Her early life was one of hardship. Her mother had died early in her life and, as the eldest, she was left with the responsibility for raising her siblings, a task that would never be forgotten by her three brothers and sister. The wedding was held in the cathedral in Tripoli and performed by the bishop of the province. After the couple lived in Athens for less than a year, they decided that they would make America their home despite the objections of my mother's family and many of my father's close relatives. My father never saw his family again. My mother, on her way to a foreign country with a virtual stranger and leaving her village life and friends behind, would not return until thirty-seven years later.

Back in the U.S., they made their way to Maryville, where I was born in June 1926, their only son. My two sisters, Helen and Nota, preceded me. In Maryville, there were only one or two other Greek families. For my mother, steeped in Greek traditions but in a foreign land and unable to speak English, it was a very lonely place, radically different from the village life she had led. Burdened with a five-syllable surname, my father changed his name to Sam Johnson. Eva became my mother's first name; it was the first syllable of her Greek name.

My father's store included Greek treats made by my mother. In a small town like Maryville, these items did not attract a lot of customers. It was hard to make a living and my parents barely eked by.

In 1931, at the beginning of the Great Depression, my parents decided to follow some of their friends and moved to Tulsa, Oklahoma, a larger city promising a better life. Oil had been discovered near Tulsa, and the oil industry's early, transformative successes led to Tulsa becoming "The Oil Capital of the World."[i]

My father had tried the sweets business with little success so he was looking for a business with more potential. After some investigating, he and a partner decided to become the proprietors of a pool hall. It was below street level at 310 South Boulder Street , on the west edge of downtown Tulsa and the only pool hall in the immediate area. They equipped it with ten pool tables, five snooker tables and one billiard table. The cues lined the walls. Customers came, picked up a cue, called out "Rack!" and, with a wooden triangle rack, my father would set up the ivory, numbered balls for play. The fee collected at the start of each game eventually grew from 10 to 25 cents. The pool hall drew the lunchtime group, and a large number of regular players who showed up daily that were skilled enough to make a living playing pool. They spent hours every day bargaining with one another. The best players gave handicaps to the less skilled. These games drew a crowd, with side-betting on the outcome. There was also one large card table for poker players. Cigarette and cigar smoke permeated the poorly ventilated building. Gambling was rampant because laws were not enforced and players found a way to circumvent them: the loser of a game would put the game stakes (fifty cents or one dollar) in one of the pool table pockets, and the winner would casually walk by and pick up his winnings. Despite being surrounded by temptations, my father never played pool and never gambled. I don't remember him even drinking beer while at work.

At slack times, I would go to the back pool table, turn on the lights and play by myself. I became what was commonly called a pool shark. I won nearly every time I played with my school friends. Sometimes we played for nickels and dimes and I earned some spending money.

The pool hall, Boulder Billiards, opened at about 9:30 a.m. and closed when the last players left, which could be near midnight. Candy bars, soft drinks and beer were sold but no food. Upstairs and a few doors down the street was the World Building, home of *The Tulsa World*, the city's largest newspaper. Appropriately, the pool hall became known as "The Underworld." It was located between two Greek-owned establishments. On one side was the 46th Star Candy Kitchen, a candy store and ice cream parlor, run by families who were influential in my parents' move to Tulsa. On the other side was The Coney Island, famous for hot dogs that would become a Tulsa legend. At lunch time, people lined the street to buy these five-cent hot dogs served with mustard or catsup, onions, and a chili sauce. Later, Jim Economou, the owner's son, would expand the business, opening several more Coney Islands in different parts of Tulsa. Eventually, all the stores were sold except the original store, now a famous downtown, historic landmark. To this day, the special chili sauce is a family secret.

Some of my most enjoyable memories from this period were the Monday nights I spent attending professional wrestling matches at The Coliseum. A family friend took me with him, since my father didn't care for wrestling. Ringside seats cost fifty to seventy-five cents. Our bleacher seats cost twenty-five cents. Because I was under twelve, I got in free, but I had to sit on the floor in the aisle. The Coliseum, a huge indoor arena on the east edge of downtown Tulsa, hosted civic events, school graduation ceremonies, shows, Tulsa's minor league hockey team's games, boxing matches, and other events; but it was the wild professional wrestling that most attracted me. Muscle-bound athletes bounced off the ropes and applied tortuous holds on their opponents, all to the deafening cheers of overflow crowds. In the late 1930s, Tulsa was a center for this type of wrestling. World championships were held at The Coliseum, attracting wrestlers from all over the Southwest.

There was and is a good deal of make-believe in professional wrestling. The matches pitted a clean, fan-supported wrestler against a wrestler playing the villain. The villain would beat up on the hero until he could hardly stand up; then suddenly, with a burst of energy, our hero would start fighting back, bounce off the ropes, and fly through the air. Cheered on by the roaring crowd, the hero would flatten his opponent. The referee would pat the mat three times and the hero would raise his hand in triumph—unless, just to keep it interesting occasionally, the villain won; then the outraged crowd bellowed its boos. What amazed me was that by the next week—with their bruises and injuries magically gone—the wrestlers were all ready to wrestle again. I believed it all. In September 1952, The Coliseum was struck by lightning and destroyed by fire. In its place now is a large apartment complex.

Those Coliseum nights were a huge and welcome contrast to my family's frugal and mostly ordinary, everyday life. When we moved to Tulsa, my father bought a small, six-room brick home with a separate one-car garage, all for six thousand dollars. It was at 1220 South Guthrie Street, some ten blocks southwest of downtown Tulsa. Until we bought our first car several years later, we walked or took the city bus everywhere.

I attended Riverview grade school, conveniently located across the street from our home. Horace Mann Junior High School, which I later attended, was a twelve-block walk, as was Central High School where I graduated at age sixteen in 1943. I loved every minute of high school and never missed a day. Central had an Indian motif: the football team was the Braves, the Tom Tom was the yearbook and the pep squads were the Scalpers and Red Feathers. The school colors were red and white. I was one of the finalists for head cheerleader but lost. During football season, noisy pep rallies were held on Friday afternoons in the school's auditorium, followed by the game that evening at Skelly Stadium. Central, with an enrollment of over 3000 students, always fielded a good team and sometimes went undefeated. Each school year ended with The Daze, a talent show staged by the students that included singing, dancing, comedy skits, and patriotic themes. I led a thirty-voice chorus in singing "Till the End of Time" and one other song. I was in a dance skit with a gorgeous, sexy girl as a partner who showed up for the performance wearing only a dark-colored, loose blouse that left her bare down to her stomach. She made me so nervous that I had a hard time keeping in step to a very appropriate dance tune entitled "Every Little Movement Has a Meaning All Its Own." When I graduated, the ceremony was held at The Coliseum. Diplomas were awarded while Elgar's "Pomp and Circumstance" was played. It was a sad time for me because my school class was breaking up—some going to war and others to far-away schools. I would need to stay home since my father was in ill health. Also, I did not have the money to go away to school, so I enrolled at the University of Tulsa for my freshman year.

The families who lived in three of the other four houses on our block each had a boy about my age. Jimmy Donahoe, who later became a famous pediatric cardiologist in St. Louis, lived on the corner, next to me; on my other side was Bobby Jones, a good golfer, full of mischief, with minor fracases with the law and, according to my mother, a bad influence on my character. Next to Bobby was Ed Moores, who went on to become a lawyer in Pittsburgh. All through high school we four were the best of friends, and we maintained our friendships for many years after graduating together.

Despite my father having legally changed our name to Johnson from Giannakopoulos many years earlier, I was still known as the Greek kid on the block. I felt different: we observed some Greek traditions. My mother spoke very broken English so she did not mix in the neighborhood. Neither did my father, who spoke English with a strong accent. When I visited or played games with my friends (Monopoly was a favorite), it was always at their houses. I don't remember ever playing with my friends in our house. Despite having close neighborhood friends, I still felt like an outsider.

Like other recent European immigrants, we never quite fit in; but my family never experienced the harsh brand of racism that led to the now-infamous race riot in May 1921, in Greenwood, the black neighborhood. About two hundred people died, eight hundred were hospitalized, thousands of Greenwood residents were arrested and thirty-five city blocks were destroyed by fire. The Greenwood riots occurred about ten years before we moved to Tulsa. In the 1930s, Tulsa's buses, schools, restaurants, and neighborhoods were all segregated—and stayed that way until after the end of World War II.

Neither my mother's differentness nor her lack of familiarity with American culture kept her from pursuing U.S. citizenship. When she appeared before a judge for her citizenship examination, she initially got off on the right foot by correctly reciting the Pledge of Allegiance (she had carefully memorized it beforehand). However, when the judge asked her, "Who is the president of your country?" she replied, "Metaxas" (the Greek prime minister). He passed her anyway.

My mother was very religious. On the east wall of one of the bedrooms in our home, she displayed our religious icons illuminated by a night lamp, its wick fed by olive oil. Her ancestry included five generations of Greek Orthodox village priests, and she wanted me to follow the family tradition. I sang in the choir and was an altar boy for several years. Then my interest in following the family's priestly tradition ended.

My mother washed our clothes, cooked our meals, and sometimes kneaded the dough to bake homemade bread—all to ensure that we lived as frugally as possible. Wonder Bread with its colorful wrapper sold for ten cents a loaf at the store—too expensive for us. So, on the way home from school, I often went by the Wonder Bread Bakery, to buy what was called day-old bread. It was actually the several-days-old bread returned by the grocery stores when unsold and then offered at the Bakery's stand for half price. This was typical of the extremes we went to, to save just five cents.

There were no doctor's bills since the medicine cabinet contained four cure-alls for all ailments. Rashes, cuts, infections, and insect bites got the iodine or Mercurachrome treatment; all body aches and pains, arthritis, soreness, chest colds, flu, sore throat, lung congestion, and others got the Vicks VapoRub or Mentholatum rubdown. A palm to the forehead served as our thermometer.

In the 1930s, during the Great Depression, beggars would knock on our front door. They were hungry and wanted food, not money.

My mother would not turn them away. She directed them to the back door, where she gave them a plate of whatever we had. After eating on the back steps, they would return the plate, thank her, and walk away. It was hard to see people suffering from hunger.

When I needed a new suit at age thirteen or so, I got a personal taste of the Depression that I still recall in minute detail. Tulsa's two downtown men's and boys' clothing stores were across the street from each other, and I shopped for my suit at both, finding one for twenty-five dollars at Palace Clothiers (somewhat like Brooks Brothers today) and one for fifteen dollars at S.G. Holmes and Sons (more like Sears). Prompted by the difference between the fabrics and linings of the two suits, I wanted the more expensive one. But my mother (the family decision-maker on such purchases) disagreed. I got the cheaper one and in a size larger, so that I would grow into it.

In 1938, when my oldest sister Helen reached her sixteenth birthday, we bought our first car, a formerly-owned 1936 Oldsmobile. Neither my father nor my mother ever learned to drive a car. So my sister drove my father to work, and we all finally rode instead of walking. Gasoline was twenty cents per gallon, fifty-five miles per hour was the highway speed limit, and there were no seat belts or turn signals on the steering wheel. To signal a right turn, you put your arm out the window vertically; for a left turn horizontally. Later, we traded the Oldsmobile and bought a new 1941 Pontiac. The following year when I turned sixteen, I got to drive that Pontiac—the first car I ever drove.

After finishing high school, my two sisters went away to school. They enrolled at Oklahoma A&M College, now known as Oklahoma State University, at Stillwater, some forty miles from Tulsa. Helen later received a degree in education and became a grade-school teacher. Nota graduated in art and later received a master's degree in art, as well as scholarships and awards for her work. She became an art instructor at Tulsa Junior College. Her paintings and etchings still hang in all of our homes and in my office.

Helen's youngest daughter Linda was our family's first tragedy. She died at age twenty-nine of cancer, leaving behind a one-year-old baby boy, Christopher. Helen adopted and raised him. He graduated from the University of Pittsburgh in 2010 and is now employed by the government in Baltimore. Helen's oldest daughter, Janet, graduated from Kent State University in education and teaches grade school in Los Angeles. Her son Steven earned his degree from Akron University in accounting and works in Canton, Ohio.

Nota was divorced and raised her two daughters by herself. Sharon, the oldest, received her Ph.D. degree in clinical psychology from Oklahoma State University and lives in Fort Collins, Colorado. Nota's second daughter, Vicki, graduated with a bachelor's degree in education at Oklahoma State and now serves as a school principal in Bristow, a small town thirty-five miles from Tulsa. Nota became our second family tragedy when she fell ill with Alzheimer's. It progressed to the advanced stage and she suffered horribly. She died in 2006.

My father never took good care of himself. He worked seven days a week and never took a vacation. In 1943, after I graduated from high school, he started having health problems. He turned for help to Radium Baths, a cure for all ailments located in Claremore, a town about thirty miles northeast of Tulsa. Sitting in a tub of dark-colored, hot, sulfurous, smelly water was supposed to be a therapeutic panacea. The water's minerals seemed to penetrate the skin, giving off an offensive smell that lasted for hours. Even though the baths took all day, my father was a frequent customer. He also occasionally resorted to venduzes, which consisted of a ball of cotton being lit by a match inside a milk glass and then quickly pressed against the part of your body that ailed you. Because the burning cotton removed the oxygen and thus created a vacuum inside the glass that made it stick against your skin, the venduza was supposed to suck the ailment out of your body. What plagued my father was far beyond the reach of these primitive treatments. The rich Greek foods making up his daily diet were plugging his arteries.

In May 1944, on Mother's Day, the lives of everyone in my family changed dramatically. My father died of heart failure at age sixty-two. My mother was a widow at age forty-seven with three young children, no job skills, and only three thousand dollars in savings. Greek funerals were very emotional, and my mother was a mess. When a family friend approached me and said, "You are now the head of your family and you are responsible for your family's well-being," my world sort of fell apart. I was only seventeen years old. I had my heart set on going to the University of Texas with one of my neighbors. However, I had money problems and too much family responsibility. Fortunately though, the following month, in June 1944 when my sisters graduated from college, they took over my mother's care and family finances. As a result in September 1944, I was free to enroll at the University of Texas in Austin—if I could afford it.

My parents' engagement, 1921.

My parents' 1921 wedding picture: why aren't they holding hands or smiling?

My two sisters and me with our loving mother, 1928.

Five years old,
with my two sisters, 1931.

Mike, Nota and Helen with our father, 1934.

Our last family photo, 1944.

COLLEGE AND CAREER
The Early Years

My years in Tulsa influenced my decision to pursue a professional career as a petroleum geologist in the oil industry. Across the Arkansas River from our home, only a half mile away, was the Mid-Continent Refinery—one of many booming oil businesses in town. When the wind was right, the air smelled like a refinery—a smell that permeated my childhood. Then in high school, I mingled with the children of rich oil families. I wanted to shape a future for myself that was as rich with possibility as their lives were. Majoring in petroleum geology, as preparation for working in the oil industry, was my key to such a life.

But first, finishing my bachelor's degree was going to be a major challenge financially. Seeking her family's help, my mother contacted her brother who had immigrated to Johannesburg, South Africa. I had never met him and my mother had not seen him for more than twenty years; however, she had virtually raised him, so he thought of her more as his mother than his sister. He had a successful bakery business in Johannesburg and agreed to help me out financially. Each month, I received a check from him for about fifty dollars. His generosity helped me through my one year at the University of Texas. I took my first college course in geology there from Dr. Fred Bullard. He so piqued my interest in the science that my destiny as a petroleum geologist was assured.

As my year at the University of Texas was ending in the spring of 1945, World War II was also nearing its end—which in turn triggered the end to my family's life in Tulsa. My sister Helen's fiancé Chris Diamant (whom she met while he was in training two years earlier at Oklahoma A&M) was due to be demobilized and would soon return from North Africa, with his bride-to-be waiting for his return in his hometown of Canton, Ohio. Having sold our interest in the pool hall to my father's partner, my mother decided that we should all move to Canton, rather than let Helen's marriage split up the family. It turned out that leaving Tulsa behind was not difficult for me, after all, since most of my high school and other friends were gone, having either moved away, joined the military, or left for a college out of town. We rented our Tulsa home to provide my mother with an income. Still, it was going to be up to me to get myself through at least my last two years of college.

A few months later we arrived in Canton, the hometown of former president William McKinley. It was an industrial town dominated by steel mills and factories and home of the Hoover Company, famous for its vacuum cleaners, and Timken, a huge roller-bearing factory where I got a job for the summer months before going back to school. I had never lived where winters were frigidly cold. Tulsa had a warmer climate and was in oil-and-gas country where gas was the common cooking and heating fuel, but in Canton we had a coal furnace. It fell to us to shovel the coal during the daytime and stoke the furnace at night.

Having completed the elementary geology courses at the University of Texas, I wanted to continue my education at a school with an outstanding geology department. I applied to the University of Michigan and Columbia University in New York. I had set my sights high. War veterans were coming home and getting preferred treatment, though. When I got rejections from both schools, I decided to apply to The Ohio State University in nearby Columbus. In-state tuition would be minimal; less than seventy-five dollars per quarter, because I now qualified as an Ohio resident. When I got to Columbus, I learned that my two years of college credits would all transfer. I started at Ohio State as a junior.

Since I wanted to join a fraternity, I went through rush week, getting bids from both Phi Gamma Delta and Alpha Tau Omega. The Phi Gams were one of the best on campus with a lot of classy guys, but a bit snobbish. I thought the ATOs would be a better fit for me, so I pledged. I got to know two other pledges, Dick Jentgen and Jake Will, and we became the best of friends. We dated the sorority girls, attended the weekly beer parties, went to the famous Ohio State football games, and rented tuxes for the formal affairs that we were somehow invited to. We went through fraternity initiation together. I was given a pill that turned my urine blue. I swallowed an oyster and it was pulled out of my mouth with an attached string. (I've never eaten one since.) We were given a wooden paddle that had to be signed by all of the members. Before signing you were asked to "assume the position" and, of course, you got whacked. I kept my paddle for many years. I still have my ATO beer mug.

Dick and Jake were both from Upper Arlington, a fashionable suburb of Columbus. Dick's father was a prominent physician and Jake's family was in the construction business. Jake was a member of Ohio State's football team, but his college career was interrupted by service in the U.S. Army. While he was away Dick and I became the best of friends. I had never had as close a friend as he was. He even moved on campus and we lived and studied together in a large rooming house with other fraternity members. A few times he invited me to spend a weekend at his family's beautiful home in Upper Arlington. Dick loved to sleep with the windows open, even in winter weather. Once, it got so cold that when I woke up, the water in the toilet bowl was frozen. We went to Beulah Park, a local thoroughbred racetrack, and won some money betting on Sonrich, a horse named after him and owned by his parents. Dick was always well-dressed and well-mannered. Some of his class rubbed off on me.

Unlike Dick, I was working my way through school. On Saturdays I worked downtown in the stockroom at the Lazarus Department Store. At the fraternity house, I peeled potatoes in the kitchen for my meals. Only later did I work at the more impressive job of lab assistant in the geology department. These differences didn't matter to our friendship. We had lots of laughs. Such was fraternity life. It was a fun time, but there was no room for idleness and I found time to study: I had to compete with war veterans who were older and more mature. I needed to make A's and B's, and I did. Some sixty-five years later, the three of us were still friends and stayed in touch with one another. Sadly, Dick and Jake both passed on last year. They remain at the heart of some of my finest memories.

Jake Will, Dick Jentgen and Mike at the ATO spring formal, 1948.

Same pose 60 years later, 2008.

Dick Jentgen borrowed my cap but I got a second degree at Ohio State anyway, 1949.

When I started my junior year at The Ohio State University, I met the most intelligent man whom I have ever known—Edmund M. Spieker, the chairman of the geology department. He had received his Ph.D. in geology from Johns Hopkins University in 1921 and started his professional career with the United States Geological Survey (USGS). In 1924, he left to join the faculty at Ohio State.

He knew something about everything. You could talk to him about any topic, and he would reply intelligently in great detail. He was fluent in German and spoke to his only son in French. As an academic exercise, he translated into English one of the earliest geological reports ever published; written in German by Johann D. Schoepf (1752-1800), the original was 194 pages in length and was entitled *Geology and Mineralogy of Eastern North America* (as translated by Spieker). He was a professional photographer and a classical concert pianist. He belonged to the national science council that advised President Truman on scientific matters. His science survey course, required for all social science majors, included physics, chemistry, astronomy and the biological sciences—and he knew them all. Some of his lectures were so awe-inspiring that students would stand and applaud when the lecture ended. He composed reports and publications tens of pages in length, in a long-hand that needed little or no editing or correction. A geology faculty member wrote that words flowed from Spieker's mind to his hand as fast as he wrote and were grammatically correct, technically accurate, and coherent. His genius required an outlet and it was alcohol. However, he was an even better lecturer when under the influence.

I never got an A in any of his classes. To him I was always a B student, and in graduate school that was the minimum grade for credit. His lectures were classic and spontaneous. His goal was to motivate your thinking process. In his exams, passing grades were not earned by memorizing data. He graded on how accurate and well-composed your answers were. "How would you respond to questioning geologic time?" or "What is your impression of the Werner theory?" were the types of questions he posed. The final exam in his graduate structural geology course was one of the crowning ironies in my college career. Before the exam, I carefully prepared for a demanding test. The course was required for graduation in my major, and the final exam counted for up to half of my grade. On the day of the final, his secretary walked into the classroom and announced that Dr. Spieker was not well and would not be present. She calmly went to the blackboard and wrote the following two sentences, which constituted the exam: "Discuss any two of the subjects taught in this course. You will be graded on maturity of thought and composition." I got another B.

Ohio State was one of the first universities to start a field station where geology was studied by observing geologic data in the field. Spieker established Ohio State's first field station at Ephraim in central Utah, his geographical area of expertise. The station is located at the west edge of the Wasatch Monocline, one of the major geological structural features of the Colorado Plateau. I attended its first session in 1947. I also attended the second session and did my master's thesis on an area near Mayfield, Utah. My geologic map of Twelvemile Canyon was the first detailed map ever made of that area. Ohio State's geology department has benefited from hundreds of master's theses and doctoral dissertations from students who attended the field camp over the last sixty-eight years. These professionally written reports are a wealth of geologic information but because nearly all were unpublished, they have not been readily accessible. The Internet solved that problem recently.

Spieker died in 1978 at age eighty-three. In his honor, I recently established a scholarship fund for qualified geology students needing financial aid to attend the Ephraim field camp. A second scholarship fund that I established is managed by The American Association of Petroleum Geologists (AAPG) for Ohio State students who are considering majoring in petroleum geology. That fund also provides, for their Geology Department Library, an online database of all AAPG publications, including memoirs, guidebooks, bulletins, and special reports totaling more than 600,000 pages.

When I graduated from Ohio State in March 1949, my fraternity and other friends could not understand how I had finished college with Bachelor of Science and Master of Science degrees by age twenty-two. My college years were fun. I had made lifelong friendships, had matured and I looked forward to a career as a petroleum geologist. I returned to Toledo where my sister lived, using that as a base to search for a job with an oil company. Since I grew up in Tulsa, the headquarters of numerous oil companies, I decided that was the place to start looking. In April 1949, I took a train to Tulsa via Chicago and checked in at the YMCA, only a few blocks from my father's pool hall. When I went to see the pool hall, I found that it had changed ownership but was the same place with the same pool tables and counters. Walking up and down past the pool tables brought back fond memories of my father and the years that I had spent there.

It was going to be hard to find a job. I decided that I didn't care where I ended up but I envisioned landing in one of the most active cities for the oil industry—Midland, Dallas, Houston, Tulsa, Oklahoma City, or Wichita (the Rockies never crossed my mind). After several rejections, disappointment set in. I had run out of companies to call on and had no interviews. I planned to go back to Ohio and schedule a second trip, this time to Dallas. Then Amerada Petroleum Corporation contacted me and granted me an interview.

My interview was with a John Ferguson. In the course of our conversation, we discovered that his son was a casual friend of mine; his son and I had graduated from high school together. I left him a transcript of my grades; I had made A's in both of the petroleum geology courses offered at Ohio State and knew that would be a plus. When our interview ended, he invited me to return the next day. At our second meeting, Ferguson introduced me to Amerada's chief geologist, A. Rodger Denison. Famous as a successful oil-finder for Amerada, Denison had held high positions with national geological societies and was active in the formulation of federal energy policy.

Amerada's earlier success can be attributed to one of the world's most renowned geologists, Everette Lee DeGolyer, who made a number of oil discoveries that guaranteed the company's instant prominence. Earlier, in Mexico, for another oil company, he had picked the location for the Portrero del Llano No. 4 well, in the Golden Lane, which produced over 125 million barrels, the greatest oil producer the world had yet seen. DeGolyer was the first to use geophysics as an exploration tool. Amerada excelled in the geophysical approach and became the most geophysically-oriented company in the U.S. DeGolyer as president, together with chief geologist Sidney Powers, brought Amerada prosperity. In the 1930s, DeGolyer left Amerada and formed DeGolyer and McNaughton, a very successful, Dallas-based, worldwide consulting firm.

In April 1951, Amerada would complete the No. 1 Clarence Iverson well, located on the Nesson anticline, in North Dakota, which ranks as one of the most important wells ever drilled in the Rocky

Mountain region.[ii] It is the discovery well for the U.S. portion of the Williston Basin. At the time, the nearest oil production was hundreds of miles distant in Kansas and western Montana. Considering the inclement weather, the distant service company and supply centers, and the lack of pipeline or refinery outlets, Amerada undertook enormous risk in drilling this prospect. Its reward was the discovery of over 500 million barrels of oil. Amerada would become one of the most highly-regarded and respected oil companies in the U.S.

Denison asked a lot of penetrating questions about petroleum geology. His interview reminded me of a college quiz. He asked if I would leave my master's thesis with him. Luckily, I had brought it with me. He finished by saying that they would review my credentials and advise me in a month or so. I returned to Toledo and started making plans for a trip to Dallas, but I received a letter from Amerada dated April 22nd, offering me a job in Casper, Wyoming at a monthly salary of $325.00. The money was fine but where was Casper, Wyoming? I had envisioned Texas or Oklahoma, but not the Rockies. In another letter, accompanying my returned thesis, Denison commented that it was O.K. but not outstanding. He also said I should understand that it would take at least a year for me to make any kind of contribution to Amerada's exploration efforts but that they were willing to take me on. What a way to begin. Taking the Amerada job was a life-changing decision and—like many others made in my formative years—it was undertaken without foreseeing its far-reaching consequences. I ended up spending my entire career in the Rocky Mountain region. I didn't drive my stake in the ground, Amerada did it for me.

Later, in May 1949, I took a train to Chicago and from there, a Union Pacific streamliner to Cheyenne and then caught a bus to

> **AMERADA PETROLEUM CORPORATION**
> BEACON BUILDING
> P.O. BOX 2040
> **TULSA 2, OKLA.**
>
> GENERAL OFFICES
> 120 BROADWAY NEW YORK
>
> April 22, 1949
>
> Mr. Mike S. Johnson
> 3103 Parkwood
> Toledo 10, Ohio
>
> Dear Mr. Johnson:
>
> As a result of our study of your credentials, and based on the interviews you had with members of our staff in Tulsa, I desire to offer you employment as a geologist for training in petroleum, to begin as soon as convenient for you. The initial salary for this position is $325.00 per month plus field expenses. In addition, we will reimburse you for the cost of transportation, food and lodging from Toledo to the place of assignment and for the cost of transporting your personal effects.
>
> The location of your first assignment will be the Casper, Wyoming, office of the company. This office has primary responsibility over Wyoming, Colorado and Montana, and your actual work might be in any of these three states. The type of work you will do will be that ordinarily assigned to men of your academic and other achievements and skill.
>
> We desire to give you adequate time to consider this offer, but due to the fact that we are considering others for this assignment, we must have your response in our hands by May 6, 1949.
>
> Yours very truly,
>
> A. R. Denison
>
> ARD:HGB

My only job offer but it included a new 1949 Chevrolet.

Casper, a town of about 23,000 people. Amerada's office was on Center Street, the main downtown street. Cowboy boots, Levis and beards were the fashion. Gambling was legal. The locally famous New Wonder Bar was across the street from Amerada's office on the main street. It had a swinging, saloon-type split door entrance, copper metal foot-rests at the bar with spittoons, and card and crap tables in the back. The call girls were upstairs. In the summer of 1949, President Truman came through Casper on a political campaign, and while he was passing by the New Wonder Bar and waving at the crowd, the ladies on the balcony responded by cheering and throwing him kisses and flower bouquets. The Old West was still alive in Casper.

I reported to geologist Charles Agey (pronounced "A-ghee"), the Casper District exploration manager, who later became my mentor. In his deep voice, he told me that I would not be stationed in Casper for long. Amerada had opened an office in Billings, Montana, and I was to begin my career there as an oil scout. How different reality was from what I had envisioned about my first job. Scouting had very little to do with geology.

My very first airplane ride was on a DC-3 from Casper to Billings. Bill Goering, the Billings manager, met me at the airport. After shaking hands, he handed me the keys to a new 1949 Chevrolet, the car that I would drive in my scouting job. It turned out to be interesting work and I loved Billings, Montana's largest city. The town, in a valley partly surrounded by rimrocks, was small and friendly. Ten to fifteen oil companies had district offices there and I quickly made a lot of friends. Amerada was admired and I was proud to be in their employ.

An oil scout is what the name implies. You gather information on the leasing and drilling activity of other oil companies. Information about other companies' leasing activities is gathered by going to the county court house, where all oil and gas leases must be recorded. Sometimes I scouted drilling activity by driving to the rig where the well was being drilled and "swabbing" (gathering information from) the roughnecks, driller, or tool-pusher (manager of the drilling crew) for any information they would share—which could turn out to be nothing. I traversed all of eastern Montana on weekly trips, staying in small towns with cheap motels, fighting winter weather and enduring the primitive nature of the Great Plains of the state.

Trading well information with other companies was another useful tactic. The simplest route to this key information was the Scout Check, the weekly meetings where all the oil companies exchanged data. Participating companies were required to release all of their drilling activity. In addition to Amerada, they included Shell, The California Company (Chevron), Carter (Exxon), Phillips 66, Stanolind (Amoco), Cities Service, Texaco, Sinclair, Continental Oil (Conoco), and others. Our scout checks were held every Thursday, and every Friday I prepared a scout report for Amerada including the latest information on all important wells drilling in Montana plus land-leasing data. I made sure to add a geologic slant to the data in my report, suggesting why these activities were taking place. This report was sent weekly to the executive office in Tulsa; they seemed pleased with my reports.

CAREER FIRSTS

As A Petroleum Geologist

Early in my career I learned how difficult it is to discover commercial oil fields. Amerada's Billings staff consisted of Jim Milor, landman, and four geologists-George Darrow, Frank Sonnenberg (father of Steve Sonnenberg, a geology professor and head of the Bakken Consortium at Colorado School of Mines), myself and manager Bill Goering. Goering explained to me that the office was opened because in early 1949, using seismic data, Amerada had completed the No. 1 Hougen discovery well for Melstone Field in Section 23-Township 10 North- Range 29 East in Musselshell County. It was the first oil producer in the state of Montana from the Tyler (Heath) Sandstone reservoir, at a depth of 4350 feet. It was destined to become one of the most important oil reservoirs in the state. The seismic data had delineated the trap, interpreted as a simple anticline three to five miles in size. Oil reserves were estimated at 3-4 million barrels. Based on past experience, Amerada envisioned development of a 15-to-20-well oil field. Amazingly, the first two offsets drilled were both dry holes. The field had a more complex and elusive geologic setting than that of a simple anticline. Finding commercial oil fields in Montana was not going to be an easy task.

In June 1950, after I had worked as a scout for about ten months, Bill Goering called me into his office. I was being transferred to the Casper district as the newest of three well-site geologists. It was hard to leave Billings: some of the friendships I had made would be lifelong. But the transfer was a promotion and learning well-site geology was essential for a petroleum geologist.

Charles Agey, my Casper boss, was not a micro-manager. He assigned the work-load and allowed you to find a way to get it done. I went out on my first well, at Sage Spring Creek field in eastern Wyoming, an oil field that Amerada had also discovered in 1949.

Well-site geology consists of examining the rock cuttings that come up from the well bore. Using a high-powered microscope, you describe and identify the rock types that are being drilled and predict the depth to the oil objective zone and how soon it will be reached. Once reached, the pay zone is examined in detail and sometimes cored. If oil shows are found, the zone is generally drill-stem tested[iii] to determine the zone's potential. When the well is completed, either as a producer or a dry hole, a final well report is written, including the well history and all pertinent geological and engineering data.

While I was based in the Casper office, one of my first projects was located in northeastern Wyoming. In July 1949, Amerada had drilled a shallow wildcat well, the No. 1 Ormesher, located in Section 35-Township 58 North-Range 68 West to a depth of 3726 feet. It was in a very remote part of the state far from any wells previously drilled. The main objective was the Muddy Sandstone, a quartz-sand reservoir which was the most important Powder River Basin oil reservoir at that time. When this well reached total depth, it surprised everyone. The Muddy Sandstone interval was totally oil-saturated. It appeared to be potentially oil-productive. It had sufficient thickness, over 100 feet to herald a sizable discovery, covering a huge area that extended beyond the limits of the acreage block leased by Amerada. To confirm the analysis that the well was oil-productive would require conducting a drill-stem test. If the test confirmed an oil discovery, Amerada was then obligated to release that information since they were members of the Scout Check in Casper. A massive competitive lease play would likely ensue. In order to keep the site information confidential, no test was run. The well was temporarily abandoned, allowing it to appear as if it were a dry hole. The plan was to re-enter the well at a later date, after additional acreage had been acquired.

During the winter of 1949-1950, as expected, rumors of the oil shows in this well led to other companies leasing in the area, but Amerada had acted quickly, securing leases on more than 50,000 acres surrounding the well. Wyoming winters are bitter cold and drilling activity at that time almost ceased because of the snows, lack of maintenance on secondary roads, and poor communications. Amerada could hardly wait for the thaw. The company was very anxious to get started on one of the best prospects in its inventory. The shallow depth, high quality of the oil, and thickness of the reservoir placed it near the top of their list of prospects. A rig had been reserved and was on hold, pending improvement in the weather and roads.

Spring came and with it the snowmelt; it slickened and muddied the roads, rendering them impassable. It was not until August 1950, that the rig was finally moved in. The well, the No. 2 Ormesher, was "spud" (commenced) that month. It was located less than 500 feet from the first well, in a more favorable spot geologically. When the Muddy Sandstone interval was penetrated, the sand grains were oil-stained, echoing results with the first well. A testing service company was called to run the drill-stem test. We took precautions in the event of a blowout or a huge oil and gas flow. Oil storage tanks were readied. During the initial and middle part of the drill-stem test, however, the results started to look inauspicious: you can sometimes predict unfavorable results before the test is even completed. When we pulled the tool out of the hole, the recovery was 960 feet of water. It was unbelievable! There was no Wonderland down the rabbit hole; there wasn't even a rabbit. We rechecked all the measurements to be sure that we had tested the correct zone and there were no errors. It was back to the drawing boards.

The results of the well made the headlines since it was being closely watched by the industry. Not uncommon in wildcat oil and gas exploration, it was another failed risk. The Casper office was asked to research the project and come up with some answers. It was at this point that I was placed in charge of this project. For the next few months, we drilled eight confidential core holes, all at shallower depths; none had oil shows. From the core hole data and the two Ormesher wells, we determined that the Muddy Sandstone (also called Newcastle) was an estuarine, near-shore, channel-type deposit varying from 30 to 105 feet thick, the porous reservoir sands occurring at the base.

Together with another geologist, I walked the outcrop of the Muddy Sandstone, along the banks of the Little Missouri River, for 24 miles. We discovered the same, thick, nearshore-type facies of the Muddy well-exposed, about one-quarter mile wide, at a legal location of NE1/4 of Section 20-Township 57 North-Range 65 West, only one mile from one of the core holes. It negated the possibility of an oil trap. Later, well data confirmed that this thick facies of the Muddy extends westward into the subsurface of the Powder River Basin traceable for more than 50 miles and is oil-productive at Recluse Field (discovered by Apache) in Township 56 North-Range 74 West.

We finally concluded that the two Ormesher wells had encountered a very small oil accumulation, covering only a few thousand feet, mixed with water. It was not commercially viable and was a bitter disappointment at a cost to Amerada of several hundred thousand dollars. The project was terminated and all wells were plugged and abandoned.

THE ARMY
A Career Detour At A Historic Moment

Just as we were finishing this project, world events occurred that would alter my career. In August 1950, the Korean War broke out when North Korea suddenly invaded South Korea. Since the end of World War II, communism was spreading and Russia, the U.S.'s former ally, was now considered an adversary. The Marshall Plan and the Truman Doctrine had saved some of the European countries from Russian communism. Similar support would now be extended to South Korea.

The military draft was still in effect, and having missed World War II, I was eligible to be drafted. It took only five weeks from the outbreak of the war for me to get my "Greetings..." notice. Despite Mr. Denison's efforts to get me deferred as a petroleum geologist (since ours was considered an essential industry), I was ordered to report for induction into the U.S. Army. Before leaving Casper, I remember reading Amerada's weekly drilling report. It included the announced location of a wildcat well to be drilled in North Dakota, the No. 1 Clarence Iverson. Several months later, it would become the discovery well for the U.S. portion of the Williston Basin and the beginning of a new oil exploration era. If I had been deferred, I would have been the well-site geologist for this well since I was the only unmarried geologist in Amerada's employ. However, it was my turn to come to bat. I showed up in Toledo and shipped out to Fort Dix, New Jersey on September 22nd for basic training.

Basic training for raw recruits began with marching drill, learning to fire an M-1 rifle (the basic army firearm), crawling under machine-gun fire simulating combat, and then bivouac (living under outdoor combat conditions). I still remember my army serial number (52004302) and performing guard duty and KP (washing pots and pans). The war in Korea was worsening and rumors were circulating that we were bound for Korea. Some men in my company got orders to Korea but I soon found that my college education would win me a preferential assignment.

At the end of eight weeks of basic training, I received special orders to report to Fort Myers, Virginia, to be interviewed and receive my assignment for the rest of my military service. Near the Pentagon, Fort Myers housed a large number of the Pentagon's military personnel including generals and admirals. I was barracked with a huge number of other college graduates. We were from schools from all over the U.S. and included law and pre-med students, engineers, science majors, accountants, business majors, and others. My interview was with an officer who queried how a college graduate with two science degrees from a major university and employed in an essential industry could not get deferred. It resulted in my being classified as an engineer and I was handed my orders to report to Fort Belvoir, Virginia.

THE ARMY: A CAREER DETOUR AT A HISTORIC MOMENT

When I arrived at Fort Belvoir it was, as it is now, a huge technical and engineering military base. My barracks was full of newly-recruited college graduates from all over the U.S. Our professional careers had been interrupted by the draft but we felt that the army was doing a good job in utilizing our talents. We helped fill the army's need for technical and administrative personnel. I was assigned to a group that taught interpretation of aerial photographs. Over a two-week course, we taught army and marine non-commissioned personnel how aerial photographs are used to construct topographic maps using three-dimension imagery derived from stereoscopes and multiplex machines, and how to identify military installations and also concealed and camouflaged structures. The army had its own way of training instructors. One basic rule was: "Tell them what you are going to tell them, then tell them, then tell them what you told them." That way the message got through. Later, after I was transferred, this group of instructors was shipped to Korea and mapped the site where the Inchon invasion occurred: very importantly, using their Fort Belvoir technology, they determined within a few feet the height of the cliffs along the shoreline where the marines landed.

In one of my classes, I met Don Hibbard, a student who was a Cal Tech graduate in geology. Our friendship grew but our contact ended abruptly when he got orders for a special assignment. Don thought that this new assignment might draw on his geologic expertise. In saying goodbye to him, I gave him my military address, just in case there was a need for more geologists.

One day, Major Alexander Pearson, serving as our group commander, called me into his office. I knew it had to be important because I had never been there before. President Truman had just fired General MacArthur, I didn't particularly like Truman, and for some reason I thought I would be getting a dressing down over something the major might have heard of my comments regarding Truman. Standing at attention, he looked at me and said, "Private Johnson, don't you like it here? I have orders in my hands to transfer you. What's the problem?" I didn't know what he was talking about and I told him so. He then said that perhaps there was a mistake and he would take care of it. However, another officer in the room turned to him and said the orders were of the highest classification, could not be rescinded, and needed to be completed in short order. And that is what happened, much to the chagrin and dismay of the major.

In June 1951, I received my highly-classified orders to report to the Navy Gun Factory in Washington, D.C. I thought that there was some mistake. It turned out to be the beginning of one of the most exciting times of my life.

When I arrived at the Navy Gun Factory, I realized that this was no ordinary military base. Fort Belvoir was very regimented: we had strict discipline, clean uniforms, shined shoes, tie tucked into the shirt. You saluted every officer you passed. Not so here. As I passed several naval officers, I dropped my duffle bag and started a salute but they waved me off. I would find that everything was informal. I still could not figure out what an army draftee was doing at the Navy Gun Factory. When I got to the building listed on my orders, I was told to go down a long aisle. I walked past a large number of navy and army officers and NCOs, sitting at empty tables talking and joking with one another. No one was working. Farther away, sitting at a corner desk was Don Hibbard, the friend who had transferred out of my aerial-photograph interpretation class. Don had learned that this project needed another geologist, gave them my name and through the army's complicated transfer process, got me transferred.

THE ARMY: A CAREER DETOUR AT A HISTORIC MOMENT

We were billeted in a naval barracks. Navy procedures and vocabulary were different: orders came over a loudspeaker ("Now hear this, now hear this"), floors were "decks," walls were "bulkheads", and doors were "hatches." "You will" was the way the sailors' daily orders began. In contrast to Ft. Belvoir, the dormitories were modern with marble floors and excellent food was served cafeteria style with appealing choices.

It began to dawn on me: this was a good deal. I felt as if I had jumped from baseball's farm teams to the major leagues. Don told me that at the moment, no one knew exactly what our project was about but that it was a high-level secret. It was currently in a waiting mode. Soon, rumors started circulating that we would be a part of a group that was going to test atomic bombs. We were going to a site that was still secret. A Class Q clearance would be required; we went through the security process. We were questioned by intelligence officers about our life history, education, and foreign travel and we were asked for references. We soon learned that we would be attached to a group called the Armed Forces Special Weapons Project (AFSWP) headquartered in the Pentagon. We were part of a technical military group that would collaborate with The Atomic Energy Commission (AEC), testing some low-Kt atomic bombs (a kiloton is the explosive force equal to 1,000 tons of TNT). We were headed for Amchitka Island off the southwestern coast of Alaska—one of the Rat Islands on the western edge of the Aleutian Range. We never learned what type of work we would be doing there. Before we were deployed, the Amchitka location was abandoned, because of its proximity to the Russian Siberian border, the inclement weather, and political overtones.

Instead, we were headed to an Air Force bombing range about sixty-five miles northwest of Las Vegas. It would become known as the Nevada Test Site (NTS), and the camp to be built would be called Mercury. The Nevada Test Site had been established early in 1950. It covers about 1375 square miles bordering Nellis Air Force Base. Located in the most uninhabited part of the U.S., it was built as a military, weapons-testing, outdoor laboratory and experimental center. It grew rapidly and by 1968 would have more than 8000 employees and military personnel, with yearly budgets of hundreds of millions of dollars.

Our wait at the Navy Gun Factory ended in July 1951. We were transferred to Kirkland Air Force Base in Albuquerque, New Mexico, a staging area for the project. Operations became very secret. Our project was not dinner conversation, and our group stayed in separate barracks. Some of the scientists and engineers in our group were in close contact with AEC personnel at Las Alamos Scientific Laboratory (LASL) where the original work to develop the atomic bomb was done. Plans were formulated for the testing that would be done at the NTS.

By this time, Don Hibbard and I had been briefed on our geologic assignment. Colonel Gordon Page, a geologist stationed in the Pentagon, would supervise our work. We were to conduct a field geology study and prepare a geologic map and report on the Nevada Test Site, concentrating on the valleys of Yucca Flat and Frenchman Flat. A detailed geologic mapping program was being planned for the entire country and our work would be a part of it, because there was a specific concern that radiation from the testing would close this area to habitation. In preparation for the testing program, the military also wanted us to determine the location of faults evident in the bordering mountains that trended into the valleys, as well as the composition of the valley-fill, the thickness of the valley-fill (or depth to bedrock), and even the temperature gradient (the rate of temperature increase with depth). These data would be integrated with other measurements to determine shock and blast effects. What was especially needed—but never found—was a large area within the valleys where the key valley-fill physical characteristics were uniform in all directions from ground zero, rather than anisotropic.

Don and I were some of the first to arrive in late July 1951. Befitting our new work, we were promoted to the rank of sergeant. In addition to our field work, we raised the flag at sunrise and lowered it at sunset, since we were at a military base. We traveled by jeep and began studying the rock outcrops along the mountainous valley margins. We visited the Groom Lake area northeast of Yucca Flat to review outcrops of Cambrian-age rocks. They are beautifully exposed and over 7000 feet in thickness, as described by H.E. Wheeler in a University of Nevada publication published in the early 1940s. It was, at the time, the only published geological report in the entire region. It was also our first encounter with rattlesnakes. Coincidentally, it is also the site of Area 51, a secret Air Force base built many years later to test future aircraft models and purportedly, to house alien spacecraft and flying saucers.

There were no base maps or topographic maps, so we worked from aerial photographs. Early in our study, two USGS geologists—Arthur Piper assisted by Joe Poole—arrived and worked with us for several days. With their help we were able to start putting together the basic geology. Nevada is part of the Basin and Range Province, one of the most structurally-complex geologic provinces in the U.S., characterized by a series of north-trending enclosed valleys separated by mountain ranges. No rivers exist so no water flows to the Pacific Ocean. The water from sparse rains remains trapped in the valleys and settles in the lowest part, forming a dry playa.

We climbed peaks to view the surrounding geology. We were probably the first white people to do so, and we found caves with Indian pottery at lookout points. The test site was a barren, dry, uninhabited desert with summer temperatures reaching 110 to 120 degrees. The hot sun darkened our skin. There was no surface vegetation in the mountains so rock outcrops were beautifully exposed. Animal life was scarce. There were no springs so we kept water in large canteens.

A few months after our field work began, three prominent geological scientists visited; they came to review and help us with our field work. Since they had spent many years in the Basin and Range in nearby areas and were experts in their field, they had been recruited by Colonel Page at AFSWP headquarters in Washington, D.C. Chester Longwell, professor emeritus at Yale, was an early pioneer in working in Nevada. In the early 1920s, using a horse-drawn buckboard for travel, he set the stage for the early interpretation of the geologic complexity of the Basin and Range. Tom Nolan, a student of Longwell's at Yale where he received his Ph.D., was the assistant director of the USGS, later to become director. Eureka was his home away from Washington, and he spent decades doing field work in Nevada. He published a USGS professional paper on the Eureka District that is still a classic. Charles Merriam, a California Institute of Technology professor, was an expert stratigrapher and paleontologist. He helped us identify and prepare an accurate stratigraphic column for the area. These three giants of Nevada geology went into the field with us, answering questions and clarifying some of our problems with the interpretation of the geology. With their outstanding help, we were able to complete a detailed study of the test site by the time the atomic testing program ended.

THE ARMY: A CAREER DETOUR AT A HISTORIC MOMENT

This unique atomic testing program started on October 22, 1951. Due to the low yield of the nuclear devices, the military would be able, for the first time in history, to conduct many tactical nuclear-effects tests. Numerous shock and heat-effect measurements were to be recorded. Models of objects made of textiles, wood, plastics and metal were placed at different distances from ground zero to measure thermal, radiation, and shock effects. These tests would provide the very first measurement data on the effects of surface and underground nuclear detonations. They would determine the response of models composed of various materials to nuclear bursts, gamma radiation amount vis-à-vis distance, and also residual radiation and contamination. Ground roll, the ground shock wave, was one of the most important effects to be measured. In addition, trigger devices were to be tested for future nuclear device production. The technical operations of these projects were headed by Dr. Athelstan Spilhaus, an inventor, geophysicist, and author of hundreds of technical articles. He was a scientific genius who fully deserved this key position.[iv]

Our project was named Operation Buster-Jangle. It consisted of six atmospheric nuclear weapon detonations and one underground shot. All were small shots, each with a yield of less than 32 kilotons. The height of the air drops was from 1000 to 1500 feet. The Army Air Force planes making the drops came from Kirkland Field. The bombs came from a storage facility in the Sandia Mountains in New Mexico. Preceding our tests was the famous Trinity shot at Alamogordo, New Mexico—the very first of the nuclear bomb detonations that gave birth to the nuclear era. It was followed quickly by the drops at Hiroshima and Nagasaki that ended World War II. The next detonation was the small Operation Ranger, the first to be conducted at the Nevada Test Site. Buster-Jangle followed. It was conducted from October 22nd to November 29th, 1951.[v]

Don and I witnessed all seven shots. They drew a big crowd. Large groups from Washington, D.C., attended, including a Massachusetts congressman named John F. Kennedy. To observe the first shot, we stood along with other technical personnel and guests, on a ridge outside the command post building nine miles south of ground zero. We wore 4.5-density goggles to protect our eyes from the flash, which was like looking into the sun on a hot summer day. When the bomb detonated, the huge white flash (lasting for five or six seconds) felt like opening an oven heated to 400°F. When the flash dimmed, the white, radiation-filled, mushroom-shaped cloud rose from the ground, churning and boiling. It was followed by a dirt- and dust-filled cloud sucked up from the ground by the blast. The wind carried the clouds northeastward away from us and Camp Mercury. There was complete silence as we waited for the shock wave to reach us, seemingly taking much longer than the estimated forty seconds. When the huge, thunderous roar of the shock wave came, it shook the ground violently like a severe earthquake. What a rare experience. How many people in the world have ever witnessed an atomic bomb explosion?

After a brief interlude in Washington, we returned and renewed our geological work in December. We wore badges that detected radiation contamination. At the entrance to Camp Mercury were showers used to wash off any radiation contamination detected.

Later, we were present for Operation Tumbler-Snapper which took place from April to June 1952. It consisted of four air drops and four tower shots ranging from one to thirty-one kilotons. In addition to testing new weapon developments, Tumbler-Snapper was undertaken to explain and correct discrepancies in the pre-test estimate and the later actual shock-wave damage in the Buster-Jangle

Operation. It also included a military exercise named Operation Desert Rock, involving 7200 soldiers. Placed in trenches, the troops were to advance after the atomic detonation, either by bus or on foot, to view the effects of the atomic blast on materials, objects and military installations placed at various distances from ground zero. It featured a tower shot with the bomb placed in a steel tower a few hundred feet above ground. Care was taken to prevent any radiation effects to everyone involved. When the countdown came, the bomb did not detonate: it misfired. Everyone was ordered to stay in their positions. All was quiet. After a few moments, a jeep started moving towards the tower. In it was a scientist who was going to disarm the device. Talk about courage. When he reached the tower, he had to climb up it because the elevator used to put the bomb into place had been removed. It was a very tense moment as he slowly climbed the tower. But he safely secured the bomb in safety mode. The troops were ordered out and returned to camp. A few days later the exercise went off as planned.

The testing program ended in early June 1952. Looking back, I have wondered, "What has science wrought on our planet?" What a terrifying destructive element had been created. The bombs we tested in Nevada are firecrackers compared with the bombs that were later built for our national defense. The shock waves of these new weapons create immense, unimaginable destruction, but even more destructive is the heat, measured in millions of degrees Fahrenheit. One bomb can wipe out an entire city.

Russia's development of the atomic bomb through espionage means started the Cold War. What preserved the peace was the retaliatory ability of any attacked country to respond. This problem is now exacerbated by rogue groups attempting to secure atomic weapons to conduct the worst horror that could be perpetrated in the world. Portable atomic weapons can destroy huge areas. This should be, and is, among the top issues to be addressed by the U.S.

The importance of such a policy was highlighted during the presidential debate in late 2008. A serious crisis had occurred in Pakistan, a nuclear power, and it appeared that the Taliban might take over part of that country. There was concern about sending in arms, or troops, or air support to aid the Pakistani government. Presidential candidate Senator John McCain was asked which of these options he would choose if he were the president. He said (not in these exact words), "None of those: the first thing that I would do is put a guard over where the bombs are."

THE ARMY: A CAREER DETOUR AT A HISTORIC MOMENT

Atomic bomb explosion, 10/22/51,
Nevada Test Site, Operation Buster-Jangle.

White radioactive cloud
30 seconds later.

On the outcrop, doing field work at Nevada Test Site, 1951.

Joe Poole, Arthur Piper and my partner Don Hibbard, who got me the Nevada assignment, 1951.

CAREER CROSSROADS

. . . and the Road Taken

In July 1952, our geological work completed, we left Nevada for the last time. On my way back to Washington, D.C., I stopped off in Tulsa. I wanted to go by Amerada's office to find out about the job waiting for me after my discharge in September. Rodger Denison had kept track of my military career and was anxious to meet with me. Charles Agey had been transferred to Tulsa and now was exploration manager for the entire Rocky Mountain region. When we met in Amerada's office, I showed them slides of the atomic explosions and reviewed the geologic report that was being prepared. Denison was impressed and even amazed at how fortunate I was to have been able to use my geologic background for my entire military service. I felt the same way.

Amerada was interested in having me back. Since my absence they had made a huge oil discovery, the #1 Clarence Iverson in North Dakota, and opened an office in Williston. They needed help there. It seemed that was where I would land.

Back at the AFSWP headquarters in Washington, I only had a few months of military service remaining, devoted to preparing a final report. It proved to be so complex that in September 1952, when I was discharged, even with all of our good-faith efforts, we had not yet completed the report. I stayed on until January 1953 in order to help finish it. Later, in 1957, with the help of the USGS, our report was published as USGS Bulletin 1021-K, entitled "Geology of the Atomic Energy Commission Nevada Proving Grounds Area, Nevada." It was the first comprehensive geologic report ever written for the Nevada Test Site area.[vi]

Leaving Washington, D.C. was hard to do. It was an exciting city. General Eisenhower had just been elected president. Winston Churchill had come to town; so had Queen Elizabeth. I had made friends with a number of people and good times were ahead in Washington. To stay in Washington, I considered changing careers and started a job search, certain that my Class Q security clearance would give me an advantage.

I interviewed with the military branch of the USGS and also with the Central Intelligence Agency. I probably could have gotten a job with either of them but those agencies could not guarantee that I would be stationed permanently in Washington; however, I might have been able to find a Washington-based position outside those agencies. It was one of those times when I had to make a life-transforming decision: either stay in Washington for the good times and big city life or return to my previous job with Amerada as a petroleum geologist in North Dakota. I decided to do the latter.

I said goodbye to Don Hibbard, who had made my Nevada career possible, and the rest of the friends I had made over the course of about eighteen months and left for Toledo. I told Amerada that

I would like to return. They replied immediately and assigned me to their Williston office. Soon I was on a Northern Pacific streamliner that made the run from Chicago to the west coast via Minneapolis. It made stops along the way, including at Williston. We arrived in late January 1953, about midnight, and it was snowing. The train station was dreary and deserted, and the temperature was below zero. What a change from Washington, D.C.

I had never been to Williston, located in northwestern North Dakota. At the time, the population was only several thousand. It is in a very sparsely populated part of the U.S.—more than 400 miles from Minneapolis to the east and Denver to the south; those were the nearest cities with a population exceeding 100,000. The state's population was only about 620,000, most of them of German and Norwegian descent. However, it has produced some interesting and famous people: movie actresses Angie Dickenson and Ann Sothern, baseball star Roger Maris, CBS news journalist Eric Severeid, and jazz singer Peggy Lee. Our 26th president Teddy Roosevelt spent a great deal of time in North Dakota; a national park in southwestern North Dakota bears his name. Several oil fields echo Roosevelt's political and personality traits, including Big Stick, Four Eyes, Rough Rider, and Bull Moose.

Amerada's huge staff based in Williston included twenty-three newly-employed geologists. Bill Goering, formerly manager of the Billings office, had been transferred and was overseeing a massive drilling program in progress. Amerada had contracted fifteen drilling rigs to develop the Nesson Anticline fields that the company had discovered in April 1951. Each geologist was assigned a rig and followed it from location to location, managing the well-sitting chores and reports. The reservoir was the Madison Limestone, with a pay zone averaging 25 feet thick, at depths of 7800 to 9300 feet. Wells took about twenty days to drill and complete. Drilling activity would continue for several years, and Amerada would become the largest oil producer in the state; the state's production would exceed 75,000 barrels per day, mainly due to Amerada activity.

As development continued, Amerada became concerned about the potential of deeper oil reservoirs below the Madison Limestone. A rig capable of drilling to a depth of 14,000 feet was contracted, and plans were to drill a deep well to test all reservoirs deeper than the Madison. I was pleased that I was assigned the well-sitting job for this important well. It was the Lars Kvam No. 2 well located in Section 19-Township 156 North-Range 95 West. Begun in the spring of 1953, drilling and testing all the potential reservoir zones took more than six months. Total depth was 14,066 feet in the Winnipeg Sandstone, the deepest known objective. Because of drilling difficulties, only the Devonian reservoir was tested and it proved to be productive. Mechanical problems slowed the progress. For me it was an all-day and all-night job. It required close supervision, so I lived in a small shack at the noisy rig-site, with a crude, two-way telephone system to relay daily well reports to Bill Goering. The winter was bitter cold.

Not everyone endured the cold winter months stoically. One Arctic-like day, a drilling crew member stopped working and started to leave the site. The drilling foreman asked him, "Where do you think you're going?" He replied, "I'm cold." The foreman said, "We're all cold." The crew member replied, "I'm going to get my coat." The foreman said testily, "Well, hurry up! Where's your coat?" "In Oklahoma."

In one three-day period, the temperature never rose above 20 degrees below zero. To prevent the water in my car radiator from freezing, I kept the car engine idling for the entire period. Williston was sixty miles away, and I only went into town to clean myself up about once a week and only then if there were drilling delays. After reaching total depth, several additional oil reservoirs were identified and would be developed in the coming years.

Shortly after this well was completed, Charles Agey called. He needed help with the overwhelming work-load in Tulsa. Without adequate staff there, important well decisions were being made before all of the well data could be gathered and analyzed. He wanted me transferred to serve as his assistant. The year before, I had been told to expect such a move once I had completed my one year in Williston and mastered what was necessary to help develop Amerada's huge asset in North Dakota.

Returning to Tulsa in February 1954 was like going home. The nearby Coney Island was still doing a wait-in-line business. I bought myself a car, rented an apartment, and settled down.

My office was next to Agey's. Down the hall was the larger office of Rodger Denison, now promoted to vice-president. On the other side of Agey's office was the office of the company's chief geologist Jack Hosterman. On the same floor were the geologic managers of the Oklahoma-Kansas District, the West Texas-New Mexico District, and the Texas Gulf Coast District. Working in the midst of all these high-level professionals, after only five years in the business, I felt as if I had made it to the top in record time. These geologic managers, together with the geophysical, land, and engineering heads, made up the executive exploration committee for Amerada Petroleum Corporation. These ten to fifteen men met weekly with

E.H. McCulloch, the president who was also a geologist. Amerada's entire exploration effort was managed by this group's weekly meetings. Everyone in the group was at the top of his field, each man having twenty or more years of experience in his area of expertise.

My job was to gather and analyze all of the data as each well was completed, so that the wells' maximum potential could be achieved. During my two years in Tulsa, approximately 280 wells were drilled and completed in the Nesson Anticline fields. Later, these fields would extend over sixty miles in length and become the largest oil discovery in the company's history.

Because of the high exploration and drilling costs, the high-risk nature of the industry and huge potential rewards, all work at Amerada was confidential. We never had lunch with explorationists from other companies. Amerada's strong foundation could be traced to its early successes in southeastern New Mexico and West Texas, where it was one of the biggest oil producers. They were greatly admired. They did not need partners and avoided joint ventures. If the executive exploration committee recommended a prospect, the company committed to the entire prospect cost.

It is in geophysical exploration that Amerada excelled, and the technical quality of its work brought the company enormous success. The most important job for Amerada's district offices was to find prospective areas where geophysical exploration would be undertaken. It was the company's exploration style to keep its seismic crews busy. No prospect could proceed to the drilling stage without first obtaining seismic coverage.

Geophysics is the most reliable, the most technical, and the most important exploration tool in the oil industry. In the 1930s, Amerada was the leader in using seismic methods for exploration, and that approach was followed throughout my entire career with the company.

Seismic maps were kept in a safe under lock and key. The seismic method of exploration entails interpreting the echoes from artificially-generated elastic waves transmitted through rocks.[vii]

One day in the summer of 1956, Charley Agey called me into his office. When he shut his door, I knew that it was something important. He told me that the Casper office was lagging in activity. Its four staff geologists, including the district manager, along with its land and geophysical personnel, made it the second largest Rocky Mountain office. Agey felt that the Casper office needed new direction and new leadership. He wanted me to move to Casper to head the geologic staff. I was stunned. What was wrong with promoting one of the staff geologists, all of whom had much more Wyoming experience than I did? It was probably a decision made by Denison at a higher level, but Agey clearly supported it. I had been in Tulsa for about two years. I knew all the upper-echelon exploration people, how the company operated and how the various departments interrelated. Amerada management wanted me to put the district on the right course; they did not have any acceptable candidates for the job among the staff geologists in Casper.

On the face of it, it was an attractive challenge, offering me an opportunity to advance my position within the company. However, sometimes when promotions are offered, you wonder if there might be a downside. What was the "catch"? That turned out to be the case here. It took only a week or two for the rest of the story—and the real challenge—to unfold. Agey dropped a bombshell: when they learned of my promotion, the entire Casper geologic staff resigned, either in support of the district manager who had been discharged or because they felt they were passed over. I was going to head the Casper office without an experienced staff. What was behind the door I was opening—the lady or the tiger?

MAJOR MILESTONES
Amerada in Wyoming

I found an empty office waiting for me in Casper. But I soon had a staff of five geologists (none with any Wyoming experience), a draftsman, and a secretary. The office also included land, geophysical, and production-engineering personnel. Amerada's Casper staff now totaled about twenty people. My job as the leader of the geological team merited a new Buick company car, an expense account and a 150-dollar raise to a total of one thousand dollars per month.

The geophysical department's seismic work was confidential, and they kept to themselves. However, I met weekly with the land department. The geological department came up with ideas and prospective areas for development. The land department would check availability of land in these prospective areas. The data was sent to Tulsa for approval. If any of the submitted prospects were approved by the executive exploration committee in Tulsa, the land department was then responsible for securing leases on those lands. Next, a complete seismic program was conducted and, if it identified a favorable drill site, it was assigned to the production department for drilling the well.

This was Amerada's seismic-centered mode of operation. Its past successes led to its adoption as the exploration strategy used in all of Amerada's district offices.

Because of its seismic expertise, Amerada was one of the first companies to attempt an oil search in the complex thrust belt of southwestern Wyoming. Thrust belts[viii] are complexly-folded and complexly-faulted areas that defy geologically accurate interpretation. The only reliable exploration tool in such areas is seismic. Amerada moved in, leased acreage, conducted a seismic program, and drilled at least one well, but with no satisfactory results. It would require the advent of a new 3-D seismic technology to unravel the complex geologic setting of thrust belts and lead years later to successful exploration efforts by the oil industry in developing oil and gas fields, some of which would be of major size.

Outside of office hours, Casper was not like Tulsa. We mingled with employees from other companies. Still, we avoided confidential company information in our conversations. The Gladstone Hotel bar became the meeting place for singles from other companies, and I soon met four men who would become lifelong friends.

I met Andy Andrikopoulos, now deceased, on the street in Casper in the fall of 1955. A Cheyenne native who had graduated from the University of Wyoming, he started in the oil business as a scout for Union Oil Company. He later did oil brokerage and oil leasing work and then launched a very successful career in acquiring and selling federal oil and gas leases. In those years, federal oil and gas leases were a bargain. They featured a ten-year term, a graduated rental cost of only twenty-five cents to one dollar per acre, and best of all, were free and clear of any title issues. Andy's financial success stemmed from his hard work and his retaining an interest in the leases after he sold them. He helped me financially when I needed it; I reciprocated by giving him good geological advice. Fifty-nine years after our first meeting, we were still good friends.

In one of Casper's old neighborhoods, I rented a house with Jerry Hill, a landman for The Atlantic Refining Company (later Atlantic Richfield). It became known as The North Casper Social Club, thanks to our many weekend parties there.

On many quiet, lonely nights in Casper, I had dinner with Wally Hardman, a landman with Stanolind (now BP). Very sincere and professional in his work, Wally was an outstanding employee and a good friend.

Jack Curtin, a Harvard and Yale graduate from Tulsa, was also a landman in Casper employed by Stanolind. His career in Casper was first curtailed by military service and then ended when he launched his own career in Houston. Over twenty-three years, he built a successful career in management and investments, concluding with his own firm, Curtin and Company. He then moved to Boston as executive vice president and chief finance officer of Cabot Corporation and later finished his career as president of Aearo Corporation, a leading provider of safety equipment.

In the summer of 1958, each of us took professional paths elsewhere. For a farewell get-together, four of us—Andy, Jerry, Jack and I—planned a river float trip up the Big Horn River in northwestern Wyoming. Joined by two other acquaintances, we rented two ten-foot, rubber, inflated boats with oars. We stocked up with enough beer, food, bedding, and cooking utensils for a four-day trip. We entered the northward-flowing river near Lovell, Wyoming for the start of a twenty-mile trip ending south of Hardin, Montana. None of us would forget the scenery, the rapids, the camaraderie, and the fishing that supplied our evening meals. Our trip almost ended prematurely when we cracked an oar while going through one of the rapids. We had no extras and worried that continuing to use the cracked oar would break it in two. Andy, known for his handyman abilities, took an axe to a fallen tree trunk, fashioned the wood into a support, and bound the cracked oar with rope. The oar made it to the end of the trip. For forty-five years it hung in Andy's office, a striking souvenir of our exciting journey. In the early 2000s, Andy and I learned that Jack was having a big birthday party. The two of us cooked up the idea of shipping the oar to Jack in Boston, hoping he would be as surprised as we imagined when it arrived. The oar remained in his possession until two years ago when I inherited it. It now adorns my office, a remembrance of good times, great friendships and fond memories.

Mike (left), Jack Curtin (2nd from left), Andy Andrikopoulos (2nd from right), Jerry Hill (3rd from right), with the famous oar, 1969.

All of us stayed in touch. I still exchange Christmas cards with Jerry, now in Sarasota, Florida, and Wally in Sun City, Arizona. Since Andy lived in nearby Cheyenne, I saw him at least monthly and we continued to be close friends.

When Jack lived in Houston, and I was there occasionally on business, he and his wife Nancy would invite me over for dinner. Our dinner-time conversations ranged from friendly chats about family topics to business issues. Jack is a wonderful person, and I treasure his friendship.

NEW PARTNERSHIPS
Personal and Professional

While in Chicago on a business trip in the summer of 1957, I visited my friend Peter Maniatis. Although Denver was Pete's home, he was attending dental school at Loyola University in Chicago. Our friendship dated back many years, stemming from our mothers growing up together in Greece.

Though I knew Pete was busy getting through dental school, I also knew that he made friends easily, so I asked him about his local acquaintances. He told me that one of his classmates had a sister whom I should meet. We decided right then to walk over to the nearby store where she worked, a fashionable women's shop called Andrew Geller on Michigan Avenue. Luckily she was there, and Pete introduced me to Kay Karras. For me it was a life-changing moment.

What a beautiful girl. She was a knockout. She was friendly, courteous, and classy. After talking only a few minutes, I was smitten.

Pete encouraged me to follow up with her. I got her address from the phone book and, on my way back to Casper I started composing a letter to her. I wrote her that I wanted to return to Chicago to take her out to dinner the next Saturday night and hoped that she would join me. I thought that it would impress her that our dinner together was the only reason I would be returning to the city. But she wrote back and turned me down.

Early in my life, I had learned to believe in perseverance: if you don't succeed, try, try again. A few weeks later (perhaps through behind-the-scenes help from Pete or someone else), I got my first date with Kay Karras. When I got to Chicago, I rented a car, picked her up at her home, and took her out to dinner. Kay was gorgeous then and still is. She was smart, sincere, and friendly, with an entrancing laugh and smile. Years later she would tell me that she was checking out my table manners and asking about my church attendance—a natural result of her attending Mundelein, a private women's Roman Catholic college in Chicago. I guess I passed. To this day, she is a well-mannered, well-dressed, beautiful, classy lady. She has also told me the real reason she married me: apparently it was my personality and the love and caring I showed for other people.

In September of 1958, the year after I met Kay, I got a career-changing call from Ted Bartling, an Ohio State classmate. In 1952, he and two others had started the Apache Corporation, a new, growing oil company that was prospering mainly from successes in Oklahoma. It was funded by Minneapolis investors being recruited by Raymond Plank and Truman Anderson, two of Apache's founders. Ted wanted to open an Apache office in Denver and wanted to talk to me about managing it.

I jumped at the idea. As Amerada's Casper district geologist, I supervised a geological staff, drafting and secretarial employees, and had land and geophysical associates. But the work was not challenging. Exploration decisions were made in Tulsa, and my staff simply provided implementing services. Though I had earned the support and recognition of the Rocky Mountain exploration manager, my next promotion was many years away. I needed professional challenges, and I wanted to move to Denver.

When Ted visited me in Casper, I worked out a three-year contract with him. It included a 150-dollar increase over my Amerada salary of $1,000 per month, a company car, a membership in the Denver Petroleum Club, a secretary, and a landman to handle the land and legal work. At age thirty-two, I was proud of my accomplishments and confident of my future success, but accepted the job knowing little about Apache's exploration style or the intense stress and pressure involved in generating its yearly, commercially-required oil and gas prospects.

During the hectic transition from Amerada in Casper to Apache in Denver, it was difficult to keep Kay's and my relationship on track. But a few weeks later, I returned to see her. Having learned that (unlike me) she loved opera, I took her to Kungsholm, a Scandinavian restaurant offering novel post-dinner entertainment: they performed opera selections on a miniature stage with music and marionettes in original costumes. Having enjoyed her favorite music first, I insisted that we next go to a noisy nightclub featuring Lionel Hampton, the king of raucous jazz. There, everyone lost their inhibitions as they danced wildly to his music, including xylophone-dominated tunes such as "When the Saints Go Marching In!" Though this was more my style than Kay's, we shared a lot of laughs that evening. We enjoyed each other's company and loved talking to one another. Our friendship was blossoming.

After many phone calls and some letters, I went back to see her again. She was the same beautiful, classy person, and we hit it off. We had common interests and were becoming closer. The day after I arrived, a Sunday, Kay invited me to her home, where I met her parents and some of their friends. When she and I retreated to the back garden, I told her of my growing feelings for her. I was really attracted to her, and I hoped that she was developing some feelings for me.

After moving in October 1958 from Casper to Denver to start my career as Apache's Rocky Mountain exploration manager, I was so busy at work that it was hard to get away. Fortunately, Kay's brother had moved to Denver to launch his dental practice and invited Kay to visit him. We connected, and I took her to the Broadmoor Resort Hotel in Colorado Springs for an afternoon outing. Our trip from Denver to the Springs was framed by extraordinary mountain scenery and enjoyable conversation. The Broadmoor lobby features expensive vintage wines on display; their dusty, faded labels invite a closer look. Somehow we got separated in the lobby crowd. When I finally spotted her, she walked right by me as if I were a stranger. I tapped her on the shoulder and said, "Remember me?" It was an embarrassing moment that we have joked about for years since. Later that evening, I told her that I loved her and hoped that she felt the same way about me.

After a few more trips to Chicago, things became serious between us. It was marriage proposal time. To this day, though, neither of us can remember what actually happened. I never came out and asked her to marry me in so many words; I just assumed that

that was where we were headed. It is the biggest decision of anyone's life, and I will always be glad that it turned out the way that it did. I bought Kay a two-carat diamond engagement ring, and we set the wedding date for early September.

My job at Apache kept me so occupied that I wrote her letters instead of visiting her in Chicago. Kay has kept them all. "Dear Mrs. Johnson to be" or "My apartment looks like an art gallery with your pictures everywhere" were some of my opening phrases. However, I still regret that I was not able to get away to attend parties planned for us by some of Kay's Chicago relatives.

Kay and her family did all the planning for our wedding. All I did was show up. We were married on September 5th, 1959, at St. Andrew Greek Orthodox Church in Chicago. Though my mother had spent the preceding year in Greece (her first time back since she married my father thirty-seven years earlier), she returned in time for our wedding.

Kay in a knockout pose, 1959.

Wedding bliss, September 5, 1959.

The wedding reception was held on the large, back lawn of Kay's parents' new home in Northfield. A string trio played classical music as it wandered through the crowd. It was an elegant affair and, most important, the start of more than fifty years of a happy marriage. The beautiful day marked the beginning of our wonderful new life together. We left the reception to spend our wedding night at the Drake Hotel and flew the next morning to Nassau.

In the Bahamas, we stayed at the Fort Montague Beach Hotel, enjoying a bar in the swimming pool, exotic fish in decorative tanks and palm trees everywhere. The beautiful beaches and warm sunshine created a perfect, peaceful setting for our honeymoon. Fifty years later we would return for our anniversary to find it an empty lot full of weeds; this time we stayed at Sandals.

On our way back home from our honeymoon, we stopped in Dallas. There, I accompanied Kay, who loves fashion, to the original Neiman Marcus. Still the corporation's headquarters and flagship store, it is now designated as a Texas Historic Landmark.

Once home in Denver, I went right back to work at Apache.

APACHE
Joining A New Breed Of Oil Company

Apache was a new breed of oil company. It was a drilling fund, one of the first. It was similar to a mutual fund except that investment was in oil and gas prospects rather than the stock market, making it a riskier investment. Some of the large investors who believed in Apache's future were also stockholders. Apache's president was Raymond Plank, who would transform Apache into greatness through his leadership. After serving as a bomber pilot in World War II, he emerged with the belief that energy would become the most important commodity in the post-war economy. He believed that a combination of high individual income tax rates (running over 80%) combined with drilling and production tax incentives would encourage highly-taxed individuals to invest in oil and gas ventures. Plank created a complex, innovative legal and tax framework for investors in Apache's drilling programs. These programs were one year in length and investors earned working interests in oil production that were burdened with operating expenses, long-term payouts and income streams lasting ten to twenty years. To simplify the process and encourage investors, Plank created a tax-free exchange of Apache program working interests owned by the investor, for Apache stock, with exchange rates approved by independent engineering and bank parties. This allowed investors to defer income tax until they sold their Apache stock at long-term capital gains rates.[ix]

In Apache's early years, three geologists also helped in Apache's rise to stardom: John Woncik, who assisted in discovering Recluse Field in Wyoming, one of Apache's first big oil discoveries; Jaye Dyer, who started with Apache on the same day that I did, rose to high office, then resigned and formed his own successful company, Dyco; and John Black, one of the best oil-finders I have ever known.

Because oil exploration programs were funded yearly, favorable results were needed each year—a difficult goal to achieve. For its services, Apache received a management fee and a small interest in the oil and gas production resulting from investors' funds. I was authorized to invest up to $50,000 in a prospect, either by purchasing oil and gas leases or by joining in a drilling venture. Utilizing my nine years of experience, I focused in the Williston Basin of North Dakota, the Powder River Basin of northeastern Wyoming, and parts of western Colorado.

Apache's strategy was to concentrate on low-risk prospects, knowing, however, that they would yield marginal oil reserves. This approach allowed for a high success ratio and looked good to investors. Only a small part of the yearly budgets funded wildcat projects with high reserve potential. With those prospects, Apache's strategy was to originate the project, buy the leases and find outside investment partners for the remaining high-risk costs.

In the late 1950s, the U.S. was not an oil importer. Domestic production satisfied the country's needs. In some states, a quota was placed on oil well production because of oil's limited market. Called "allowables," these quotas limited oil production to ten to twenty barrels per day in some areas. They affected the economics of oil ventures because they restricted cash flow and extended the payout period. Gas also had its problems. In some states it was not even marketable, so it was flared. I remember a picture hanging in an Amerada petroleum engineer's office that read, "Gas is the bastard offspring of the fervent search for oil." That would soon change with increased oil prices and a concomitant demand for natural gas.

By 1960, some companies, including Apache, began turning to gas exploration. Ahead of the crowd, Apache became gas conscious. Demand for gas rose so rapidly that by the mid-1970s it would reach a crisis level. We began looking for gas reserves, and western Colorado had some promising geologic settings, including the Piceance (pronounced "pea-ontz") Basin. A large portion of that basin was calculated as being gas-bearing. Drawbacks included the gas price (only thirteen to fourteen cents per thousand cubic feet), no available pipeline to the Denver market, and the water production associated with the gas. The only major gas pipeline in the area was the Northwest Pipeline System, but it was nearly at capacity already, with gas from the San Juan Basin. What was needed was a pipeline across the Front Range into the Denver market. Rocky Mountain Pipeline Company, based in Denver, was considering such a project.

In spite of these drawbacks, Apache decided to go forward. We leased or optioned over 100,000 acres and drilled two wells. The first one drilled, the discovery well for Plateau gas field, was commercially productive. The second well, drilled in October 1960 and located on top of Grand Mesa, was drilled to a depth of 7545 feet at an unbelievable elevation of 9900 feet. It was a dry hole. Later, gas prices did not rise, the pipeline was never built, and the gas producer—which had found only a limited market—did not last. The project was abandoned. Today, however, most of the Piceance Basin acreage that Apache controlled in the 1960s is gas-productive, as a result of new drilling technology. Shire Gulch and Plateau gas fields contain over 200 recently-completed gas wells. In the oil and gas exploration business, launching an exploration project too early, when all the economic and technical requirements have not yet been met, is just as bad as drilling failures. We were there too early.

One of the few bright spots in my Apache career was a small oil discovery in the Denver Julesburg Basin of eastern Colorado. We named it Pat Field. It consisted of only two "J" sandstone reservoir oil producers but with very good oil reserves.

In 1963, after five years of struggling, Apache closed their Denver office. I was asked to move to Tulsa and manage the Rocky Mountain operation from there. By then, I had a lot of Denver friends and contacts, and did not want to transfer. Fortunately, Apache put me on a part-time retainer for 250 dollars per month, allowing me to stay in Denver. In the next two years, Apache would discover the Recluse Field, one of the largest oil fields in the Powder River Basin. This would help propel them to new heights, setting the stage for Apache to later become one of the most successful and most highly-regarded oil companies on the New York Stock Exchange and in the U.S. My only regret is that in my five years with Apache, I did not fully repay them for all that I had learned about becoming an oil-finder and tackling the oil business aggressively and intelligently. My Apache years were not my finest hour.

Ted Bartling (seated), Apache's first
employee, with Raymond Plank,
Apache Oil Corp. founder, 1953.

Raymond Plank and Mike, 2012.

LAUNCHING A CONSULTING CAREER

When I started my consulting career, I moved into the Patterson Building across the street from Apache's old office. Apache gave me all their office furniture, which amply filled my small, two-room office. The Patterson Building was full of oil people, some of whom I already knew. At that time, oil company offices were still scattered throughout the Rocky Mountain region, in cities such as Bismarck, Billings, Casper, and Salt Lake City. Denver had not yet become the oil capital of the Rockies.

To get my new career up and running, Kay helped out financially. In Chicago she had been a buyer for Andrew Geller and with that experience, she was able to get a job at Neusteters, a fashionable women's clothier in downtown Denver. That helped pay the bills.

When times were slack, I took well-sitting jobs, at 75 dollars per day plus expenses. Once, in April 1964, when I was desperate, I agreed to do a three-well, 20-day-long, well-sitting job for Zoller-

Danneburg in North Dakota for the bargain price of 900 dollars. It was, at best, a break-even venture.

But even an unprofitable venture was preferable to a nightmare adventure, like the one I had on my drive to a well-sitting job on a bitter-cold, winter night in a remote corner of northeastern Wyoming. I had passed through the town of Moorcroft and on to the D Road, a locally-famous dirt road developed by the early pioneers. Snow was deep and driving was hazardous. On a stretch of ice, my car slid into a ditch. Spinning the wheels only deepened the hole. It was pitch black except for the rig lights that broke the darkness about a mile away. The rig had a phone but I didn't. But I had a warm coat and gloves, so I started walking in the ankle-deep snow. I had not gone more than 300 yards when I saw someone walking towards me. All by myself and miles from nowhere, it startled me. There was talk that some mountain men in this area lived in upgraded caves—and more than lived up to their reputations as extremely misanthropic loners.

I wondered if he might be armed. It was one of those hair-raising moments when you suddenly realize that you might be facing a life-changing event—or even a life-ending one. It was frightening when he approached, stopped close to me and stared. In a menacing voice, he wanted to know what I was doing walking in the snow at nighttime on the D Road. I told him about my car in the ditch and how I was headed for the rig for help. He said he had a phone at his place nearby that I could use and ordered me to follow him. Suspicion set in and I needed to make a quick decision, weighing both my reservations and my circumstances: it was a mile to the rig but much closer to his place. So I reluctantly backtracked with him, passing my car and trekking on a few hundred yards farther to his place.

It was a rundown shack. What was inside was even worse. There was no flooring, it was just dirt with dead sagebrush matting; it smelled, and it was filthy everywhere I looked. There was a single light bulb for light and the only heat was a wood-burning fireplace. He said, "Come over, stand bah the far'." When he took off his coat and hat, I got a good look at him. His dirty, unshaven face was capped by a ring of dirt at his hat line; above that he was clean. He had not washed for days or weeks, possibly because of the lack of fresh water.

He showed me to the phone near the fireplace and next to a bundle of clothes on the floor. The bundle started to move. It was a woman in a sleeping bag. She had just given birth and the baby, no more than a few days old, was cradled in her arms, making soft cries. What a pitiful sight. While he opened some canned food for her, I asked him if I could be of any help to either of them. None wanted, I didn't ask for details, made my phone call, thanked him for his help, and walked back to my car. I felt as if I had time-traveled to the tough frontier days of yester-year. The truck from the rig came and pulled my car out of the ditch, and we drove to the rig. When I got home later, I thought about turning my benefactor in to the county health authorities but doubted there would be anyone who dealt with situations like his.

Those early hardscrabble days came to an end when a fortunate series of events helped launch my consulting career. They all stemmed from a golden opportunity for oil speculators in the 1960s—inexpensive, highly advantageous lotteries held for leases of federal lands.

Millions of acres of federal lands are located in some of the oil-producing sedimentary basins in the western U.S. In one of the biggest bargains in the oil business during the sixties, the Bureau of Land Management (BLM) offered unleased federal lands with a clean title, cheap yearly rentals, and a ten-year term for lease at monthly drawings. They were eagerly sought after.

All interested parties paid a ten-dollar fee to place their names in the box, a drawing was held, and the lease was awarded. Since a few of those leases were quite valuable if you could identify those with maximum potential, the lotteries drew thousands of applicants. Many speculators played the lottery and sometimes were successful in winning a prized lease. Some of these prized leases sold for thousands of dollars, plus the lease winner would reserve an overriding royalty interest[x] that assured him or her of an oil and gas income if the lease proved productive.

I put Kay's name and mine in the lottery for two years with no results. But finally in 1965, Kay won a 640-acre lease in southeastern New Mexico, an active oil-producing area. It had attracted more than two thousand applicants, due to its value. We quickly sold it, reserving an override, to Franco-Western (a company I had never heard of) for seventy-five dollars per acre, totaling $48,000. Our total cost was less than eight hundred dollars. It paid our entire year's living expenses.

Our good fortune continued when, only six months later, Kay won a second lease (I never won any) in the same New Mexico area as her first; it too sold quickly for a similar amount. Then, a few years later, good fortune graced us again: wells drilled on these leases discovered gas, and we received monthly royalty checks from the operator. Forty-nine years later, we are still receiving those checks albeit in much smaller amounts. Government policy soon changed and the lottery system was abandoned and replaced by oral bids, which ended the speculators' ability to acquire cheap federal leases. Oral bidding continues to this day, providing the federal government with millions of dollars of revenue yearly.

THE GEOLOGIC STUDY GROUP

In 1963 I was invited to join The Geologic Study Group. My fellow members included twenty-four men—mostly consultants, college professors, or members of small oil firms. The group was started in 1954 by Bob Berg (who ultimately became chair of the Geology Department at Texas A&M) and John Donnell, a USGS geologist. This group of geologists traditionally meets on the third Tuesday of each month. Each member takes a turn at hosting the meeting and speaks on a topic related to petroleum geology. There are few guest speakers. There are no officers, no by-laws, no assets, no dues or bank accounts, not even any stationery. One member, Bruce Tohill, handles the annual Christmas party and another member, Ira Pasternack, now succeeded by Robin Swank, sends out a list of the year's speakers and at each meeting announces the next month's program and any other pertinent information. In 1999, we broke the gender barrier by adding female geologists. Currently, there are forty-seven members (eleven of whom are emeritus), including six women. Counting past members, some seventeen have served as president of the Rocky Mountain Association of Geologists (RMAG), and many of us have won awards, authored technical papers, and chaired or served on committees for symposiums, conventions, and important regional meetings. The Group is outstanding in its collective high-level accomplishments and in serving the industry. One of our outstanding members, John Robinson, served as general chairman of the Annual National AAPG Meeting held in Denver in June 2015; more than 6000 members from over 100 countries attended.

In July 1999, as co-editors, Mark Longman and I, together with seven other Study Group members, published *A Bibliography of Rocky Mountain Oil and Gas Fields*. This was a painstaking task of assembling some 1500 articles on 1100 Rocky Mountain oil and gas fields taken from bulletins, memoirs, guidebooks, symposiums, and reports of the various geological societies and state and federal agencies. It was published in RMAG's *The Mountain Geologist*. Updated five years later, it remains an excellent research reference.

Monthly meetings are outstanding. Because of the professional audience, speakers spend considerable time preparing for their talks, which are nearly always timely and interesting subjects. There is a second geologic study group in Denver with the same name with which we have yearly joint meetings.

Among the retired former members of our Group is Don Todd, who had a phenomenal career. In 1964, he recognized the oil potential that existed in far-away Indonesia, but which was at the time under communist influence. His study revealed a large number of excellent oil fields onshore, all producing at a shallow depth, which he believed trended and extended into the huge, shallow, undrilled, offshore waters of Java. After negotiating with Indonesian officials from 1964 to 1966 in a dangerous political atmosphere with unbelievable patience, persistence, and against great odds, his company IIAPCO (Independent Indonesian American Petroleum Company) was awarded the first ever offshore Production Sharing Contract. The contract entitled IIAPCO to explore 14 million acres offshore northwest Java. Outlasting and out-negotiating some of the major oil companies, it was later awarded another 32 million acres offshore southeast Sumatra. After many turndowns from oil companies while seeking financing, IIAPCO found a buyer by merging with Natomas, a shipping company. The merger was a tremendous success, resulting in the discovery of huge oil reserves. Since the beginning of production in 1971, more than 3.6 billion barrels of oil and gas equivalent have been produced. The contract that IIAPCO signed with Indonesia became a worldwide model, changing the legal relationship from a colonial concept of a concession to one of production sharing; a more realistic partnership between a host nation and a foreign investing company, it is still in use today.

Don's was one of the most classic talks ever given at the Study Group.

OBSCURITY TO SUCCESS IN THE OIL BUSINESS

Mike with co-authors of *A Bibliography of Rocky Mountain Oil and Gas Fields*.

With successful international oil pioneer Don Todd.

WESSELY-HEADINGTON YEARS

Exploration Success

Meanwhile, Apache's chief geologist, John Woncik, alerted me in 1967 that he had given my name to a Dallas friend who was interested in hiring a consultant to generate oil and gas prospects in the Rocky Mountain region. His Dallas friend was Arthur Wessely, president of Wessely Energy Corporation. That was the beginning of a wonderful professional relationship that lasted more than ten years.

I met with Wessely later that year at the Oklahoma City airport. Looking like an executive despite his young age, he was a fast-talking oil geologist who had already excelled at finding oil and gas in the mid-continent. He enjoyed a good reputation in Dallas and was backed financially by Buddy Fogelson, prominent oilman, owner of a huge New Mexico ranch, and the husband of movie actress Greer Garson, who sometimes accompanied him at his Christmas parties.

Wessely agreed to my two key demands—that I would work for him part-time (since I had other ongoing projects) and that I would earn an override in any oil or gas that I discovered. We settled on 2%, the usual figure. I also received a $750-per-month retainer starting January 1, 1968. I felt like Santa Claus had just come down the chimney. This, together with my small Apache retainer, would pay for all my living and business expenses. I had a backer for any drilling deals that I generated. I looked forward to the challenge.

A few weeks later, Clare and Edward Headington, brothers and co-owners of Headington Oil Company, walked into my office. They were joining Wessely in the Rocky Mountain venture as his partners. They proved to be two of the finest oil people whom I would ever meet. In their Oklahoma City offices, Clare handled the finances and raised the drilling funds, and Ed did the geology. Clare's son Tim would later become the president of the family company, overseeing the development of a Montana oil field that sold for more than a billion dollars. Ed, a bachelor, was very close with his brother's family. He was extraordinarily meticulous, methodical, and careful in scrutinizing drilling prospects. I had never met two more courteous and kind gentlemen in the oil business. We would develop a long-lasting friendship.

My new consulting career capitalized on my original work in northeastern Wyoming's Powder River Basin. The area was gaining prominence as an oil province, and activity was increasing. I had studied and researched its two main oil-producing reservoirs, the Muddy Sandstone and the Minnelusa Formation[xi] and constructed maps outlining potential drillable prospects. I began concentrating on two prospects in the vicinity of Gillette, one of the largest towns in the basin; I named them Clabaugh and South Bishop Ranch.

They both targeted the Minnelusa reservoir, an unconformity-type oil trap. Now came the tricky and risky business of expertly analyzing a number of geologic factors in the hope that a viable, drillable project would emerge.

Clabaugh was based on a lone Minnelusa well drilled by Shell several years earlier, with oil shows located in Section 35-Township 48 North – Range 71 West. No other wells had been drilled there. I interpreted it as lying on the edge of a large Minnelusa oil accumulation. The acreage was not leased so we leased over 2000 acres surrounding the Shell well.

South Bishop Ranch was an entirely different type of prospect. It was located in Section 25-Township 48 North-Range 70 West, between two Minnelusa oil fields; Bishop Ranch, located a few miles northward, and the huge Dillinger Ranch field, a few miles southward with produced oil reserves of over 14.7 million barrels and 1.58 billion cubic feet of gas. The geologic oil-trapping factors for this prospect were present, but we had one problem: after we had purchased conventional leases on 960 acres and secured a drilling option on another 160 acres under lease by Chevron, one key 160-acre lease—an open federal lease—remained unavailable. A few months later it was included in a federal drawing. Several hundred applicants filed for our key lease, including Kay and me. The winner was a woman named Bumgardner who lived on a ranch outside Cheyenne, Wyoming. Immediately after she was declared the winner, I got her phone number from the operator and called her, negotiated some terms and subleased the lease from her. It was not too soon. Other companies called her later to buy the lease and then called me. I felt that we had a good prospect.

We located a rig and decided to drill both wells together, with Clabaugh first. I did the well-sitting. It was a disappointing dry hole.

The marginal well that Shell had drilled was the limit of the oil accumulation. When time came to drill the South Bishop Ranch Prospect, Ed joined me. The well was named the No. 1 Bumgardner, located in Section 25-Township 48 North-Range 70 West. He wanted to be present when we reached the Minnelusa pay zone. I again did the well-sitting. In most cases drilling operations slow down. Here, minutes turned into hours and sometimes into days. We reached the pay zone, and the rock cuttings from the well bore came up heavily oil-stained—a positive sign. We decided to run a drill-stem test to determine the zone's oil potential. Ed, however, was running out of time and had to leave to return home. When Ed got to the Casper airport, he called and I told him that fluid was entering the test tool but we did not know whether it was oil or water. When he got to Denver, he called again. I told him that I thought that we had an oil discovery but we still did not know its extent or whether it was water-free. When he landed in Oklahoma City, I gave him the exciting news: we had a water-free oil discovery probably capable of producing 500 or more barrels per day. Wessely called and offered congratulations. Clare was pleased; Ed was overjoyed. We made the front page of *Petroleum Information*, the largest oil news publication in the Rockies.

We officially completed the well on August 6th, 1968, for 610 barrels of oil per day. I had envisioned and implemented the entire project: I had come up with the geologic idea; I had sold Wessely and the Headingtons on drilling the well; I had leased all of the acreage, including the key Bumgardner lease, and negotiated the Chevron option; I sat the well, and I represented our group at the spacing hearing held in Casper before the Wyoming Oil and Gas Commission. We were granted 80-acre spacing, allowing us to drill three more successful wells. However, the geologic data suggested the possibility that the field was not fully developed with our existing wells. One more well drilled one-half mile from the already-producing wells could turn out to be either a dry hole (and thus fully define the limits of the field) or a productive well that might double the field size to ten wells. Wessely-Headington elected not to drill it.

My first monthly royalty check was for 4200 dollars, many times my monthly income. This successful venture would lead to more drilling by our group.

In 1977, some nine years later, Wessely-Headington received a record-breaking offer and sold all of their interest in the field to Polumbus Petroleum Corporation. This made for a story interesting enough to merit a quick detour.

Jim Bowden was the pumper for South Bishop Ranch Field. He was hired by Wessely-Headington to visit the field daily to record oil, gas, and water production and do any cleanup that was required. One day I ran into him in the field and he told me that Tenneco, operator of the huge Dillinger Ranch Field adjacent to South Bishop Ranch, was having a production problem. They had injected 320,000 barrels of water into a water-injection well to create a waterflood to stimulate oil production but with no effect. The water was going elsewhere. Polumbus had followed this activity closely from data available at the Wyoming Oil and Gas Commission. They believed that the injected water was charging the undeveloped part of South Bishop Ranch that I had earlier recommended to Wessely-Headington. That idea is what prompted the record-breaking offer. Polumbus quickly drilled the extension that I had earlier recommended and successfully extended the field size to eleven wells.

I decided to sell my overriding royalty interest to Polumbus (on terms comparable to Wessely-Headington's) and received a check for $160,000, the most I had ever made on one project. I was so pleased at the closing that I stopped on my way to the bank to make a copy of the check at a copy shop, so I could frame it. When I arrived at the bank, I discovered that I had the copy but had left the check at the shop. I believe I broke the record for the 100-yard dash, racing back to find my check still in the copy machine.

The cumulative production for South Bishop Ranch now stands at 5,170,378 barrels. The Bumgardner discovery well produced 818,641 barrels and is now abandoned.

Over the next few years, Wessely-Headington joined in drilling several more of my prospects. Some were commercial successes but none as profitable as South Bishop Ranch.

FAMILY LIFE IN DENVER

Kay and I started our lives together in Denver at my apartment in east Denver, close to the University of Colorado Medical Center. Moving to Denver was a challenge for Kay, who had left her family and all of her lifelong friends in Chicago. After the Loop's frenetic pace and high-flying cultural scene, Denver's downtown must have seemed like a backwater to Kay in 1959.

We decided to build our first home in Littleton, a southern Denver suburb that was filling with tract houses. In June 1960, we moved into a tri-level, one of five choices available. It would be a few years before the entire house was fully furnished. Since we opted for add-ons (bigger windows and a patio door), our house cost $22,000; thanks to my G.I. loan, the monthly payment was only $162.

The next summer we took a vacation through the canyon lands of Utah and Arizona. It was Kay's first trip through the West, and I planned it to capitalize on the magnificent scenery and sights. It turned out to be unforgettable. After driving to Vernal, Utah on the first day, we drove through the San Rafael Swell, one of the undiscovered wonders of the American West. It is a gigantic, scenic, barren dome of multi-colored sandstone and shales, covering an area of 3000 square miles.

From there we went to Bryce National Park. Despite its often being called a canyon, it is actually a series of giant, natural amphitheaters formed by frost-weathering and stream erosion of the sedimentary rocks, spectacularly displayed in innumerable shadings of red, orange and white.

Zion National Park, fifty miles westward, is a breathtaking 125,000 acres. An awe-inspiring network of colorful canyons, forested mesas and striking deserts, the Park is one of the largest preserved wildernesses in America.

Our most isolated stop was next, at Goulding's Trading Post, Utah, near the Four Corners, the only place in the U.S. where four states (Colorado, New Mexico, Utah and Arizona) meet at a common corner. Started as a post for trading with the Navajos, it later became a tourist attraction because of its spectacular desert scenery. Several western movies had been filmed there, since the Post's setting and buildings authentically represented the frontier. Those include "The Searchers," "She Wore a Yellow Ribbon", and "Stagecoach." The only telephone, which tapped into a primitive two-way system, was located in the motel lobby of the only motel; everyone waited their turn to make a call. We had planned to stay two nights but had second thoughts when we found four daddy-long-legs crawling up and down the drapes in our room. Even though they were harmless, we called the owners who quickly scooped them up and dropped them outside. On our way to dinner, hundreds of squealing, ugly bats hovered overhead, devouring insects by the thousands. Kay was ready to move on, but there was nowhere else to stay. At our family-style dinner—with everyone helping themselves from big food platters placed in the center of the table—we sat next to a New York couple who had never traveled in the West; they were astounded at the wild landscape and the vastly different culture of the Navajos as explained by their tour guide. There was yet one more surprise when the lights went out for the evening: wolves howled throughout the night. We left the next morning for the Grand Canyon.

We were glad that we ended our vacation at the Grand Canyon, the epitome of natural grandeur. Powerful and inspiring, its immense size overwhelms the senses: one mile deep, it measures some eighteen miles wide from rim to rim and lengthwise can be traced for 250 miles—a world-renowned and truly breathtaking site.

Mike and Kay, Grand Canyon, early 1960s.

A few years later, we traveled to Yellowstone National Park in northwestern Wyoming. Though few visitors realize it, Yellowstone is a non-conical type of volcano; it is the largest volcano of any type in North America. Forty miles wide, this colossal volcanic hot-spot houses a huge cauldron of magma. Its cataclysmic eruption several hundred thousand years ago left a layer of volcanic ash—a grey, gritty, claylike rock, five to ten feet thick—as far away as eastern Nebraska, a distance of about six hundred miles. Yellowstone is not extinct. The geysers and hot springs that tourists see today are the muted surface indications of the danger that lies below.

On the way home, we passed Crowheart Butte, a famous landmark en route to Lander, Wyoming. I told Kay the story of how the butte got its name: in 1866 a battle was fought there between the Bannock-Shoshone Indians and the Crows over the Wind River valley hunting grounds. To avoid bloodshed, the tribes agreed that only the two chiefs, Chief Washakie of the Bannock-Shoshones and Chief Big Robber of the Crows, would fight for the rights to the contested land. When the Bannock-Shoshone chief killed the Crow chief, he celebrated his triumph by cutting out the heart of his enemy and eating it. In utter disbelief, Kay said, "You mean he ate his heart?"

Over the years, Vail, Colorado has become one of our favorite vacation spots. We started going there forty years ago and we never seem to tire of its beautiful mountain scenery. Vail, known as one of the outstanding ski resorts of the world, is also a beautiful place in the summer with spectacular wildflowers, mountain settings, and the famous Betty Ford Alpine Garden Center.

Every year, "American Days" is celebrated over the Fourth of July holiday in observance of the signing of the Declaration of Indepen-

At Vail American Days celebration, July 4, 2015.

dence. It is part of a festive thirty-day series of events that includes performances by the New York, Philadelphia, and Dallas Philharmonic Orchestras, chamber music, string quartets, famous violin and piano soloists, and others.

The American Days festivities begin in late morning with a typical, small-town, Western parade featuring grand marshals, bands, cowgirls and ponies, rodeo royalty, dogs, and pickup trucks and cars representing restaurants, auto body shops, baby-sitting agencies, auto-consignment companies, and plumbing and heating establishments. Plus a 1966 Pontiac, a man running for the office of County Coroner, and kids tossing candy to the hundreds of parade watchers standing or sitting in lawn chairs. There are some fifty other parading participants, all welcomed with lots of noise and cheers.

Later, Vail Valley Foundation and BRAVO!VAIL present a splendid concert held at the Gerald R. Ford Amphitheater, with seating for 1260. Twenty-dollar tickets are only available the morning of the concert and are gone by noon. A grassy hillside provides free access for 1300 more.

The crowd, waving small hand-held American flags, joins the Dallas Philharmonic Orchestra in singing patriotic Sousa selections. Patriotism continues to swell, as the musicians segue into the swing music of World War II's famous Glenn Miller Band and, with veterans standing amid loud applause, the signature songs of each branch of the U.S. military. The concluding performance of Tchaikovsky's 1812 Overture ensures that everyone leaves the concert with an uplifted, patriotic feeling for our wonderful country.

Capping the end of the festivities is a spectacular fireworks display. The many patriotic souls who travel from Denver for the celebration seem eager to return year after year, despite bumper-to-bumper traffic all the way back home, 110 miles away.

FOREIGN ADVENTURES AND INTRIGUES

Venturing into foreign oil exploration has always been intriguing. In the 1960s, after the easy-to-find oil in the U.S. had mostly been discovered, companies were looking abroad for the big oil targets. By the 1960s the Emirates in the Middle East had changed from feudal states to wealthy countries. Downtown Dubai, soon lavished in oil wealth, took on a look like mid-Manhattan. It has one of the largest shopping centers in the world and includes an aquarium three stories high and about one city block long, holding 33,000 fish. It also has a 162-story office building and the only 7-star hotel in the world. When you fly their airlines, they take you to the airport in a Rolls Royce. As for natural gas, Qatar and Iran are two of the world's leaders in gas reserves, but Russia comes in as number one.

Europe (especially the North Sea), North Africa, and Central America also became popular targets. Only six years into my consulting career, I began my first foreign venture.

In 1969 Ed Headington called and asked me to review an oil and gas prospect in the Republic of Panama that had been submitted to him, launching yet another interesting adventure. Robert J. (Bob) Pinder, a Salt Lake City resident and president of U.S. Silver and Mining Company, had obtained an option on three large acreage blocks in the Chucunaque Basin, in Darien Province of eastern Panama. The geologic report showed that the geologic setting was favorable: a thick Tertiary sedimentary section[xii] appeared to be present. Its one outstanding feature was a well drilled by Cities Service Oil Company in 1926 that had tested oil. The published data showed that the well was capable of producing 4000 barrels of warm salt water per day from a sandstone reservoir 110-feet thick at a depth of only 3500 feet. The water recovery had an oil cut of 10%. That's 400 barrels of oil a day. For whatever reason, Cities Service did not follow up on this oil show. No more drilling had been done. It was possible that the Cities Service well had penetrated the oil-water contact at the edge of a field and that at a higher structural position, we would find the reservoir water-free, resulting in a potential of thousands of barrels of oil per day.

With the extraordinarily high costs involved, oil exploration in frontier areas and foreign countries requires especially rigorous analysis of the three factors important for any successful venture—a source, a reservoir and a trap. In this case, we knew the source was present since oil was recovered on the test. The 4000 barrels of water per day, 10% oil, certainly indicated a high-quality reservoir. What was missing was information on the trap's size.

Since Pinder's company, U.S. Silver, was a public, penny-stock operation, a successful discovery of this magnitude would send the stock soaring. Dollar signs danced in our eyes. Ed decided to pursue the venture a little further, while I investigated the important Cities Service well data and verified the oil recovery. Searching some old publications at the University of Colorado geology department, I discovered that the data was accurate and the prospect was in an area with a geologic setting favorable for oil accumulation.

The concession terms were similar to terms of other frontier, foreign concessions. There was no front-end cash bonus or drilling obligation. The government reserved a one-sixth royalty (16.667%) on all hydrocarbons produced, and the lease term was for twenty years with variable options for further extensions. The acreage consisted of three blocks totaling 275,000 hectares or about 675,000 acres. Annual rentals averaged only sixteen cents per acre—a total of $108,000.

After conferring with Clare, Ed thought that it would be worth the cost of a trip to Panama to find the well and examine the area first-hand. We planned a trip with Pinder to locate the well site if it could be found, do a quick test of the well, determine the road access, and research the area's geologic suitability for a favorable drillsite. Meanwhile, we also negotiated some substantial U.S. Silver stock options with Pinder. The plan was to fly to Panama City, take a chartered plane to La Palma, the capital of Darien Province, and then take a boat up the Yape River to the village of Yape. From there, we would walk through the jungle to the Cities Service well site.

Our contact man in Panama was Tony Sossa, Bob Pinder's friend. He knew the government officials and had set up meetings for us to discuss terms, since favorable licensing terms and government cooperation were necessary to facilitate our exploration efforts. We also had to minimize the security risks stemming from the heavy drug traffic streaming over Panama's border with Colombia. We were provided with two Panamanian army bodyguards, armed with submachine guns, to escort us for the entire trip. Fortunately, when we returned to Panama City, the bodyguards still had their original supply of bullets.

One other issue was the fer de lance, a coral snake and an extremely poisonous member of the viper family, found in forests and jungles of tropical America. They were plentiful in this jungle, so we had to be on constant guard to avoid getting bitten: any bite would be fatal.

Bob Pinder, Ed Headington and his nephew Tim and I got shots for malaria before flying to Panama City. At a local store, we stocked up on groceries and other goods for the scheduled four-day trip to the jungle. We were all equipped with high-top boots and double-padded pant legs.

We chartered a one-engine plane, a de Haviland Beaver, to La Palma. After landing, we transferred our gear onto a large piragua, an engine-driven canoe-like boat, and got on board.

Arriving in Yape, Panama: guard, pilot, Sossa, Pinder, Tim and Ed Headington. Photo by Mike Johnson, 1969.

I had never been in a jungle, and Darien's is a rainforest, with lots of rain and with parts of it impenetrable. At the time, the Pan American highway extended from Alaska to Argentina, except for the most challenging section—the impenetrable jungle in Darien. What struck me the most was the jungle's eerie quiet in the daytime, contrasted to its nighttime noise: the jungle was alive with unseen nocturnal animals. The snakes worried us most, since large, thick branches overhung the river. Fortunately, we never saw a snake during our entire trip.

After arriving in Yape, we settled our gear in the school house that was to serve as our base. The next day our group of seven left afoot. Fortunately, not long into our walk, we encountered an elderly man who claimed to know the Cities Service well's location.

The density of the lush rainforest growth was amazing. Though we could follow existing trails, we had to cut our way through some of them. After walking for a few hours and by a stroke of luck, we came upon the Cities Service well. A 75-foot palm tree was growing just a few feet from the well's "Christmas tree" (the surface pipe equipment). Using tools he had brought with him, Bob Pinder broke open the connection of the well's shut-in valve. A stream of water shot out fifty yards or more. It was gassy and smelled of sulfur but not oil.

But we now knew that the well was no fairy tale. There were no rock exposures so field work was not possible. Plant material five to ten feet thick covered the ground. The surrounding jungle revealed more trails but no roads. We took pictures of the wellhead and the surrounding landscape, returned to Yape, and prepared to leave the next day for Panama City. The same one-engine plane that brought us to Yape was waiting. I looked down the clearing that was the runway. It was nothing but uneven, matted jungle vegetation less than a half mile long with high palm trees looming in the background. The seven of us, including the two armed guards, sat in two rows with one long seat belt per row. When the pilot told us that the short runway was not one of his favorites, we looked at one another in concern and wonderment. It is occasions like this that might prompt some bystander to say, "Before you take off, do you owe any of us any money?" We did get off safely but once airborne some dark rain clouds loomed in front of us and we had to veer towards the Pacific Ocean to avoid the storm. It was a bumpy, scary ride all the way to Panama City. The two armed guards, experiencing their first air flight (unlike the rest of us) thoroughly enjoyed the entire trip.

Headington was not interested in funding the entire drilling phase of the project, so we needed outside financing. For our prospect proposal, I prepared a report covering the project's geology, economics, concession terms and other data. It included two pluses: the nearby Refineria Panama, a buyer of oil products, and offsetting concessions owned by Exxon and Mobil. These companies would be prime candidates to help fund our project in exchange for our technical and well data.

Our goal was to find a company willing to drill two wells to depths of 3500 and 5000 feet—one near the Cities Service well and a second to be located on the Quebrado Sucia Dome, a five-mile-long anticline uncovered by library research; these two were considered the best prospects in the area. Over the next few months, our Darien prospect proposal was shown to ten to fifteen companies in Houston, Dallas and Denver. But we faced unexpected setbacks—a sudden change in Panama's government and internal problems between U.S. Silver and Headington. We also soon exhausted the list of oil companies involved in international exploration without generating either sufficient interest or outside financing. A few months later, much to our disappointment, the project was abandoned.

In the last several years, a serious attempt has been made by the Panamanian government to start an oil and gas exploration program in Darien. Scattered international oil news reports have appeared that estimate Darien Province's potential at hundreds of millions of barrels. A Colombian operator, Harken de Panama Ltd., reportedly initiated discussions with Panamanian government officials about granting them a Darien concession but negotiations failed. Though Panama announced in 2011 that they would be offering oil and gas concessions through bidding, no formal requests for bids have appeared. Doing business in Panama will be difficult due to government red tape, alleged corruption, the daunting jungle landscape and topography, and the lack of a large, nearby market. However, the project's geologic merits are still tantalizing.

Another foreign venture I was involved in was launched in 1995. It began with a meeting in Houston with Ted Bartling. He had left Apache long before, spent some time with Ada Oil Company (owned by Bud Adams), and then gone on to other ventures. We had kept up a relationship for some 32 years since my Apache days. I had done some consulting work for him and we had stayed in touch. He wanted me to meet Gene Van Dyke, owner of Vanco, a Houston-based company. It had operations in the North Sea, the most important oil province in Europe. This led to my first venture there.

At the time, I was doing consulting work for DEP, the Greek National Oil Company in Athens. DEP was interested in getting involved in foreign projects and had hired me to review both projects submitted to them and ones that I originated. Greece lags behind other European countries in oil development; Prinos-Kavala, in the northern part of the Aegean Sea, is Greece's lone commercial oil and gas field. Discovered in 1981, it has produced 116 million barrels of oil and currently produces only 2000 barrels per day. Gas production from the nearby Kavala gas field totals 28 billion cubic feet and current production is only about one million cubic feet per day. Recent reworking of the field by Energean Oil Company has increased remaining reserves at Prinos to 30 million barrels. The northern Aegean Sea has additional oil potential; however, government red tape and politics have thwarted oil exploration in Greece for years. Even Albania, bordering Greece on the north, produces more—over 19,000 barrels per day. Oil seeps have been known since 400 B.C., as reported by Herodotus. My first recommendation to them, however, was that they fly to nearby Tripoli or Cairo and review projects there. Libya was a major oil producer and Greece did not have any political problems with them. Egypt was an up-and-coming country with great potential. In 1996, Apache would discover Qarun Field in the western desert that would attain production of over 11,000 barrels per day. Supported by my geological reports and recommendations, these two ideas moved through the layers of bureaucracy in Athens but were quickly dismissed for political reasons. Instead, they were pursuing a trade project with Iran—trading fruits and vegetables for crude oil.

When the Tripoli-Cairo initiative failed, I went to Vanco's office with Ted Bartling and met Gene Van Dyke. Ted wanted me to review one of their prospects located in the Netherlands portion of the North Sea. I quickly determined that this prospect had a great deal of merit and that it might suit DEP. Vanco had an almost unbelievable set of geologic, seismic, engineering, and well data in the Netherlands portion of the North Sea. This database gave them an advantage since these detailed files and maps included data overlooked by others, and revealed important information that upgraded the project, named the P-8A Prospect. It was a major-sized gas prospect with reserve potential of over 730 billion cubic feet of gas. It encompassed a ten-mile-long, faulted anticline covering 6095 acres and targeting the Bunter Sandstone reservoir, 600 feet thick, at depths of 8500 feet. Projected total depth was 10,500 feet in the Lower Permian. Shallow rights, already productive, were reserved by other companies. Well cost was estimated at five to ten million dollars. Projected spud date was November 1995.

Vanco was seeking investors in P-8A Prospect to pay for the cost of drilling the exploratory well. Investors would pay for 100% of the cost of the well but earn a lesser percentage in interest; the difference (called a carried working interest) would remain with Vanco.

One of the first potential investors that Vanco contacted was Occidental Petroleum in Los Angeles; having enjoyed enormous success in Libya in the 1960s, it was a prime candidate. If it would commit to taking a 25% interest, Vanco would be well positioned to sell the rest of the prospect to others. Vanco also had Amoco and Hunt Oil Company in mind as potential investors.

I reviewed the prospect and determined that it had a great deal of merit. I submitted the prospect to DEP.

DEP was interested in foreign projects but DEP's makeup was not suited to handling oil operations in foreign countries even as a non-operator. A better fit for DEP in P-8A would be for it to buy an overriding royalty interest, if one could be created, with a one-time payment, thus avoiding any operational and monthly billing costs. I contacted Vanco and they appeared to be interested in the idea since it would give them cash, and Vanco could recoup some of its cost in the project. This proposal prompted a trip by DEP personnel to Houston to meet with Vanco, review the prospect in detail, and discuss terms.

Meanwhile, Vanco got some good news. In reviewing P-8A, Occidental's interest was piqued and they decided to take the entire prospect. The agreed-to terms were that Occidental (or ONI for Occidental Netherlands, Inc.) would earn a 55% interest in P-8A for paying 100% of the cost of drilling the first well. Vanco had hit a home run by so quickly finding a company like Oxy that would take the entire interest.

DEP was headed by Teresa Fokianou Malaveta. She was a good administrator but—along with her staff—lacked experience in evaluating foreign wildcat prospects such as P-8A. The few days they spent in Houston went well, and they advised Vanco of their continued interest. They returned to Athens with high hopes of proceeding. Wanting additional input, they hired a consulting group in London to review the prospect and give an independent evaluation. It was favorably approved. In Athens, I was asked to meet with a Greek air force brigadier general, an ex-fighter pilot, who was on the advisory staff of DEP. At lunch, he quizzed me about P-8A. I found that he knew less about the oil business than I knew about fighter planes. Companies in Denver were also reviewing the project, including the William Obering Companies and Tatex Energy.

Finally, in discussions with Teresa Fokianou Malaveta, I recommended the project to them again, while taking into account and advising them of the risk inherent in wildcat projects such as this one. They needed approval from the next political level above them. What had impressed them the most in P-8A was Occidental's overwhelming interest and the fact that they would be the operator.

DEP received permission to commit to the project. In subsequent meetings in Houston, DEP finalized an agreement with Vanco, whereby they paid cash for a 2.5% overriding royalty interest in the entire prospect. Obering and Tatex also invested in the project. For finding Vanco an investor in P-8A, I received a cash commission and a small override.

The well spud in late 1995. The drilling went well and quickly. Vanco's daily drilling reports were eagerly followed and DEP had high hopes for success. Success would launch an extended exploration program for them. Gene Van Dyke's daily comments were always positive. The phrase "running high and looking good" accurately summarized his comments. But when total depth was reached, there were no shows of gas. Disappointment set in and the well was plugged and abandoned. The failure was attributed to the trap-forming faults not sealing the trap. In Greek fashion, failure had its consequences: Teresa Fokianou Malaveta was replaced, and DEP was reorganized. Since I had gotten my DEP consulting job through a connection I had with a now-retired cabinet officer with PASOK (the governing party in Greece), I then moved on to other projects.

Toasting the P-8A Prospect, North Sea, with Gene Van Dyke, president of Vanco

Still another one of my foreign consulting jobs in the 1990s was for Philip Anschutz, who had taken charge of Anschutz Drilling Company from his father. He had occasionally called on me to give him an opinion on oil prospects submitted to him by other companies. I believe that he respected my analyses and ideas. He had even offered me a position but I had already decided that I was going to pursue my career as an independent consulting petroleum geologist.

Anschutz's sterling career has spanned beyond the oil business into western art, entertainment, real estate, sports, medical facilities, railroads, fiber-optics, and other enterprises. Denver also knows him as one of the city's premier philanthropists. His varied holdings included the Anschutz Ranch located in Utah's northeast corner, in a thrust belt. Previously, only ten miles south of the ranch, Occidental Petroleum had discovered Pineview, a thrust-belt-type oil field that has produced over 32.6 million barrels.

Anschutz resisted the many legitimate, attractive offers from major oil companies to lease his ranch and, displaying his typical nerve for ventures fraught with risk, opted to develop it himself. The result was the discovery of East Anschutz Ranch oil field, a major oil field (which to date has produced 129 million barrels). Later, he sold a half interest in the field to Mobil for half a billion dollars. By the 1980s Anschutz was a billionaire. In the 1990s, he was also looking for more thrust-belt deals. I knew about one in Greece.

Western Greece is a 120-mile-long thrust belt. It contains good source rocks and high-quality reservoir rocks (two important requirements for wildcat exploration), plus oil seeps, where oil has oozed out of the rocks onto the surface, a positive sign. But there is a problem: it contains thick layers of salt and salt diapers (plugs) in the subsurface, complicating seismic interpretation.

In the early nineties, I presented a summary report on this area to Ted Weller, Anschutz's foreign exploration manager. He passed it on to Anschutz and they agreed to move forward. I would lead the effort. It was up to me to put the project into a geologic perspective, select a favorable area, help negotiate the project with the government officials and ideally, later, with additional geologic and seismic work, come up with a drill site. Everything was subject to Anschutz's approval.

I felt more confident tackling the government negotiations because I had a key partner, Everett J. Athens from Tulsa. Not only did our family connections date back to our roots in Maryville, but Everett had fought with the Greek guerrillas against the German occupation forces in World War II, forging friendships with guerillas who later rose to high positions within the Greek government. One of his best wartime connections was with John Tsouderos whose father, Emmanuel Tsouderos, was prime minister of Greece in exile until the war's end. John and Everett served in the same unit during the war and had remained close friends. With his connections to government officials, politicians, ship-owners, and other important business people in Athens, John was an attractive choice as our representative in Greece; he became responsible for helping us in our attempt to obtain an oil and gas concession. Our agreement was that I would handle the science, while Everett and John would handle the negotiations and the political problems.

We targeted the most promising part of the thrust belt, in the province of Epirus in the northwestern corner of Greece where it borders Albania. Joining me in the field work were Greek National Oil Company (DEP) geologists, headed by Deno Nikolaou, and Anschutz's Dietrich Roeder and Doug Lindsey.

Over several years encompassing many trips to Greece, we reviewed published geological reports, conducted field geology reconnaissance, visited the famous oil seep at Dragopsa, met with government officials, and finally selected the province of Epirus as our primary target.

Though Greece was slow in developing concession terms, by 1997 the government had finally conceded to terms standard in agreements of other foreign countries. It would be a sealed-bid sale, with each interested oil company's bid enclosed in a folder with the terms of its offering: royalty amount, size of acreage block requested, the planned exploration program (including seismic work), the drilling program, and other details. On a specified day, all offers would be opened and reviewed and the company with the best offer would immediately be awarded the concession. On the day that the sealed bids were opened, Anschutz made the highest bid but the concession was awarded to another company through questionable means. It was an embarrassing moment for me, a costly one for my friends at Anschutz, and a disappointment to all.

The company that was awarded the Epirus block, Enterprise Oil and Gas Company, conducted a seismic program and drilled one well that failed. They soon relinquished their holdings. In 2012, fourteen years later, Energean Oil Company (with minor partner Petra and technical partner Schlumberger) filed for and was awarded the same block. They have announced plans to drill several wells. As recognized by Anschutz many years earlier, it is a complex but attractive prospect.

No new, large oil discoveries have been reported in Greece, and exploration activity has been minimal. However, in 2014, the Greek government announced the offering of a licensing round in 2015 for parts of the Adriatic offshore in western Greece extending southward to the southern offshore of Crete. In January 2015, a change in government canceled this offering.

Any oil or gas discoveries would be a boon to Greece's economy. The recent crises in Greece's economy and the ripple effects in the European Union have created havoc. Greek citizens typically were not paying their taxes, taxes received by the government were not being applied to their intended use, and the nation's debt had reached astronomical proportions. It will require a great deal of sacrifice to settle Greece's economic problems.

During my career, I was also involved in several other failed foreign ventures, in Turkey, Guatemala and Ethiopia. My experience in foreign ventures tells me that they have huge potential, but are difficult to assemble, fraught with problems (changes in government, marketing, environment, taxes and other issues) and are best left to the major oil companies and large independents that have the expertise, technical ability, and financing to explore them.

OUR FAMILY BLOSSOMS

Alicia, born in 1965, and Mark, four years later, are our two children. Alicia was a beautiful baby. Until she was eight years old, she was very shy. I took her to Y Indian Guides, a father-daughter neighborhood program with five to ten other duos. We sat in a circle, donned Indian headdresses, gave everyone an Indian name, and focused on developing a father-daughter bond. As I look back, it was one of my most enjoyable experiences; we still have the Indian headdresses. After Alicia finished high school, she attended Fort Lewis College in Durango, Colorado and received two degrees, one in English and one in Theatre. She decided to live in the mountains—a natural choice given her love of skiing. Later, she enrolled at Metropolitan State College in Denver, majoring in computer science. Also for many years, she was a substitute teacher at various schools in the area where she lived. She showed exemplary concern for her pupils with learning disabilities, staying after school to help them. Years later, these students have returned to thank her for her assistance.

She met Michael Pierce on a ski run in 2007 and they married in 2010. Their wedding was a well-planned affair attended by 200 guests. The reception was held at the Grant-Humphreys Mansion, now designated as a historic site. We were entertained by a classical string trio, a jazz dance band, and a Greek duo for Greek folk dancing. Alicia was beautiful and radiant in her wedding gown and Michael beamed throughout the whole affair. They left the reception with the top down in Kay's red BMW convertible, with Alicia's bridal veil flying in the air. The reception continued late into the night. From the start Kay and I liked Michael, particularly for his kind and courteous manners and the way he treated our daughter.

Alicia and Michael are excellent skiers, having mastered the black runs and moguls. They have a home in Evergreen, Colorado, and both a condominium and a house in Fraser, near Winter Park, Colorado; they love their mountain style of living. They have taken exotic trips to New Zealand, Italy, St. Martin, Chile, and to the Turks and Caicos islands. They tolerate the deer that jump their back yard fence and eat their shrubs and flowers, and they hike the nearby mountain peaks. Kay and I also have a condo in Vail, which provides them access to some of the best skiing in the world.

Alicia now serves as the very efficient office manager of my LLCs in downtown Denver, and Michael manages my investment portfolio. Alicia has a friendly nature and is at ease in making friends. She knows more people in my office building than I do. I have come to be known as Alicia's father, not the other way around. Alicia and Michael are a wonderful couple, happily married and enjoying life together.

Mark was very active as a youngster. It was fascinating to watch him solve puzzles and play with others, usually taking the role of their leader. But he drove his mother to distraction with his endless energy. One day, when he was about four years old, we took him to a nearby ice skating rink so he could burn off some of that energy. As soon as we got a pair of rented ice skates on his feet, he took off in a blaze and has been skating ever since. After discovering ice hockey, he played all through high school and into college. I attended not only his games, but also most of his practices. He has also passed the hockey tradition on to his children.

Mark excelled scholastically as a youngster and was admitted to Kent Country Day School, where he spent the last six years of school. He took advanced courses in some subjects and helped academically challenged students, but, most important, he learned how to concentrate and study.

As a young teenager, he mowed lawns in the neighborhood, saved money and bought parts for and assembled an early-model computer. We knew he was bright and that he would succeed in any endeavor he chose.

Mark attended the University of Colorado (CU), majoring in engineering. While there, he met and married Judy Vocke, a beautiful woman and a welcomed addition to our family. A graduate of Louisiana State University, Judy was working in Denver in interior landscaping. Not long after Mark graduated from CU with a degree in engineering, he and Judy became proud parents of their first son.

Thanks to Mark's academic achievements in college, he got a job immediately after graduation with a firm founded by his academic advisor at CU. He was assigned to the company's Orlando, Florida office and moved there with Judy and their son. Judy was employed by a telecommunications company and so excelled at managing others that she was offered a job supervising several hundred employees.

But the position was in Fort Lauderdale. They decided to make the move; Mark quit his job, and they relocated to nearby Boca Raton, where they live today.

After a short stint with a small engineering firm in Boca Raton, Mark started his own company, Johnson Structural Group. By the time their second son was born in 1995, Mark's company had grown enough to add several engineers. However, the 2008 recession took its toll on his work. Loyal to his staff, however, he fired no one. The economy rebounded after a few years and, with it, his work. One of his projects was a 600-bed, nine-story dormitory at Miami International University and another is a 220,000-square foot, retired-living complex. Judy now serves as the office manager of their company. The Johnson Structural Group is well-known and respected in Boca Raton. A superb cook, Judy enjoys preparing Mark and the boys' meals typical of those in the best restaurants. Mark, Judy and the boys are a closely knit hockey family. Mark still plays hockey in a league of older players. Judy is a marvelous mom for the boys.

Our two grandchildren are Mark and Judy's sons. Justus Michael Johnson (also called J. Michael or Jay) is twenty-four years old. I was at the hospital in Denver when he was born in January 1992. After Judy and Mark first held him, they gave him to me. I had never held an infant only thirty minutes old. He was still blinking his eyes, getting acclimated to daylight. In high school, J. Michael took an advanced and rigorous schedule of courses for four years. He left for school at 6:00 a.m., returning home at four in the afternoon. He earned good grades, including some college credits that helped prepare him for his current engineering studies at Clemson University. We are proud and lucky to have him as our grandson. He plans to follow his father into the engineering field.

Hunter, now twenty, graduated from St. George's School in Rhode Island. Like his father, he started playing hockey at age five. He made the A Team as a "mite," the six-year-olds' class, and has competed at that level for his entire hockey career. We have attended his tournaments in numerous cities, where he has played against teams from as far away as Europe and Russia. We have enjoyed them all. In addition to being an A student, he was the only freshman to make St. George's varsity hockey team and was team captain the following two years. He is an exceptionally good hockey player. Hunter's parents flew to Rhode Island to watch him play, just as they go to Clemson to see J. Michael and to attend football games and homecomings. We are confident that he has a bright future ahead of him in college.

No account of our family life would be complete without including Homer, our beloved dog, a ten-pound Maltese born in 1999.

J. Michael, Mark, Kay, Mike, Judy and Hunter, Florida, 2009.

The dogs that preceded him—a Tibetan terrier, a Weimaraner and a Llaso Apso—were ordinary, compared to Homer. We had trained him early, and he seldom had accidents. He was a bundle of joy for Kay. He lived his entire life at our condo on Yosemite Street. Our homeowners' association required that dogs be on a leash, and he knew the rules we taught him. Kay loved to take him for walks, as he sniffed the entire neighborhood. We knew some neighbors only by their dog's name.

When we left him alone in the house, we gave him a treat, and he quietly waited for our return. When we returned, he would bark loudly, wagging his tail, licking us with his tongue, welcoming us back. He gave us undying love.

If Kay had ailments and needed comfort, Homer was there for her. He would lie quietly by her bedside for hours just as lap dogs do. We flew him with us to Florida, and he quietly slept in the kennel at our feet throughout the entire trip. But he disliked being groomed and trembled when we took him for long car rides.

When he was ten years old, he started having heart problems. We were told by the vet and the heart specialist that he would last for another six months to a year. His heart problem later was complicated by lung and liver failure. Under veterinary care, he survived for two years, until 2012.

The saddest time for us was when we had to put him down. Kay and I drove to the vet's office. She stayed in the car. I took him in, took off his collar and tags, and the vet put him to sleep. It was a sad, emotional event, but it is the price you pay for the privilege of having a beloved dog.

OUR FAMILY BLOSSOMS

Alicia, 8, and Mark, 4, in 1973.

Y Indian Guides, Alicia and her father,
ca. 1975.

Grandparents Elaine and Evangelos Karras with Alicia and Mark, ca. 1972.

Our happy family—Mark, Kay, Mike and Alicia—in 1977.

OUR FAMILY BLOSSOMS

Mark, the hockey player.

Skiing with Mark and Alicia at Vail in Colorado's beautiful mountains, 1983.

Beloved dog Homer, 1999-2012.

THE CHURCH
A Major Commitment in Philanthropy

As an earth scientist, I marvel at God's wonders—mountains, deserts, oceans, canyon lands, and famous sights such as the Grand Canyon and Niagara Falls. More recently, a miracle of modern technology demonstrating the unbelievable expanse of the universe: on July 14, 2015, a fly-by of the American New Horizons probe past the planet Pluto was completed, at a speed of 30,800 miles per hour, passing within 7800 miles of its surface. Launched in 2006, it took nine years to travel three billion miles and with bull's-eye accuracy!

My wife and I are church-goers, and I also have volunteered my services to help with our church causes and administration. This work led to my appointment in 1974 to the Archdiocesan Council, the largest and most important laity group of the Greek Orthodox Church. The Council is headed by the Archbishop, whose advisors within the Council include the metropolitans of the eight metropolises and about one hundred lay appointees. This council offers advice and services to the Archbishop on finances, human rights issues and problems affecting Hellenism and Orthodoxy in the U.S.

At the first Council meeting that I attended in Chicago, I was impressed by the quality of the handful of laity members who functioned as its inner circle. They all were successful businessmen who had served on the Council for many years, were well informed on the issues, and were relied on extensively for their advice. However, Archbishop Iakovos, a born leader and a brilliant and eloquent theologian, outshone them. He is the first person I have ever met who struck me with genuine awe. A hushed silence greeted his entry at the Council meeting. Accompanied by an entourage including his very efficient assistant Paulette Poulos, he slowly made his way into the meeting room, pausing to greet those waiting in line to see him. His opening remarks to the Council were classic and inspiring. They set the tone for a two-day discussion of church issues. He excelled as a leader. His mannerisms and character compelled everyone to follow his lead.

Well-known in national and international religious circles, he defended the human rights of the oppressed across the globe. Once, a group of us accompanied him to the White House to meet with President Jimmy Carter about the Cyprus crisis. In persuasive, emotional words, he strongly defended the rights of Greek Cypriots and pleaded for the help of the U.S. government in protecting them. However, not much was achieved, and years later the crisis still exists.

In his thirty-seven years as Archbishop, he consecrated hundreds of churches and chapels and received honorary degrees from more than fifty colleges and universities. He was the first clergyman to offer the invocation at the opening session of both houses of Congress. He was invited to the White House and offered advice to all the presidents from Eisenhower to George H.W. Bush, primarily on human rights issues. He served as president of the World Council of Churches. He received hundreds of awards, plaques, trophies, medals, and other honors, all displayed on the second floor of the library of Holy Cross Seminary (the only Greek Orthodox theological school in the U.S.) in Brookline, Massachusetts, outside Boston. The library is named in his honor.

One of the highlights of his career was on June 9th, 1980, when President Jimmy Carter awarded him the nation's highest honor for a civilian: the United States Medal of Freedom. He was the first Greek-American to receive this prestigious award. He was one of five honorees (some represented posthumously by others) including opera singer Beverly Sills, playwright Tennessee Williams, Vice President Hubert Humphrey and movie actor John Wayne. Kay and I attended the ceremony at the White House. A small group of us then attended a dinner with entertainment by the U.S. Marine Band, followed by a large reception on the West Lawn, looking out towards the Washington Monument. It was a very elegant and deeply touching affair.

We returned to Denver the next evening in time to watch the late TV news. A short news clip featured the five honorees, with His Eminence standing in the center, holding his staff. The blowing wind only enhanced his natural prominence. It was a great day in America for Greek Orthodoxy.

Archbishop Iakovos retired in 1996, the same year I concluded my twenty-two years of service on the Archdiocesan Council. His obituary made the front pages of the *Wall Street Journal* and the *New York Times* when he died in 1998. He is buried behind the chapel of

Holy Cross Seminary. I continue to support church affairs through my membership in Leadership 100 and FAITH, two church charitable organizations.

In 2009 Andy Andrikopoulos and I traveled to Constantinople (Istanbul) for an audience with His All Holiness Patriarch Bartholomew, leader of the world's 300 million Eastern Orthodox Christians. Our luncheon appointment with him was cancelled when he was suddenly hospitalized with influenza. We visited Saint Sophia Cathedral, built in the sixth century, formerly the Orthodox equivalent of the Papal Basilica of Saint Peter in Rome. For more than nine hundred years, it was the largest cathedral in the world until it fell to the Muslims (led by Sultan Mehmet in May 1453), which marked the end of Byzantium. The beautiful ancient iconography in the cathedral is now mostly masked with white plaster and Muslim symbols are everywhere. It is currently a museum and the largest tourist attraction in Turkey. We had the good fortune of having dinner that evening with the crew of "60 Minutes," which was producing the twenty-minute segment on the Patriarch and his church that appeared on CBS on December 20, 2009. He outlined in detail the hardships that Eastern Orthodoxy has endured under the Turkish government. Since then, very little progress has been made.

For the last sixteen years, the Greek Orthodox Archdiocese has been headed by Archbishop Demetrios, an outstanding theologian, who deserves a great deal of credit as the leader of the more than 525 Greek Orthodox parishes in the U.S. One of his greatest accomplishments and legacies, however, will be the St. Nicholas National Shrine at Ground Zero, currently under construction in lower Manhattan, New York. A spectacular forty to fifty million dollar structure, it replaces the small Greek Orthodox church destroyed in the terrorist attack September 11th, 2001. It will not only serve as a parish but will also include a quiet, non-denominational bereavement center; a place for meditation for all faiths honoring the victims of the terrorist attack. Because of its location, it is expected to become one of the outstanding tourist attractions in New York City that millions of people will visit every year.

Mike and Kay at a church meeting in New York with
His Eminence Archbishop Iakovos, 1985.

With Andy with His All Holiness
Patriarch Bartholomew, 2009.

AN INTERLUDE
WITH THE RUSSIANS

When Denver hosted the 57th Annual Convention of The American Association of Petroleum Geologists (AAPG) in April 1972, I was responsible for recruiting speakers to report on new oil and gas discoveries and advances in petroleum geology in foreign countries. I thought that a Russian speaker would be a highlight for the Foreign Section talks. Surprisingly, the Russian Institute of Geology and Exploitation of Combustible Fuels in Moscow agreed to send three representatives: Dr. N.A. Eremenko, Director of the Institute, would speak and two additional scientists would attend. Dr. Eremenko had visited the U.S. before but this was the first trip for the other two, Gurgen Ovanesov and Vladimir Semenovich.

As chairman of the AAPG Foreign Section, I met them at the airport and saw them to the Brown Palace, their hotel. I also planned two trips for them, one to the Marathon Oil Company Research Laboratory on South Broadway in Denver and the other to the U.S.

Geological Survey facility at the Federal Center in Lakewood. Dr. David McKenzie, a good friend, showed them around the Marathon facility; Reuben Ross, also a close friend, guided them through the offices and labs of the USGS. Eremenko did not seem very impressed with the projects that he was shown, indicating that Russia had similar projects that matched our progress in these areas. He also claimed that Russia had set world records in deep drilling, ranging below 20,000 feet. When the four of us met with AAPG president Sherman Wengerd and they were subsequently interviewed by *The Denver Post*, their poor English skills hampered our conversations.

AAPG Annual Convention, Denver, 1972, with the Russians.

Walking to the convention meetings one day in a crowded downtown area, we passed a man perched on top of a stool, yelling in a loud voice about some political issue. He was drawing a rowdy crowd. A police officer was standing nearby. They asked for an explanation. I told them that the police officer was there to protect the speaker, who was exercising his right of free speech. They found that strange, given the contrast with what would happen in Russia under the same circumstances.

Coincidentally, this convention was held at the same time as the flight of Apollo 16. When Apollo 16's landing on the moon seemed threatened, we all—including the Russians—followed TV news coverage closely day by day, even hour by hour. It was a stressful time for all Americans, and I was impressed by the Russians' sympathy and concern for the astronauts.

I invited them to my home to see where I lived. Along the way, I pointed out local streets, parks, and shopping centers and drove through my neighborhood. When one of them asked me to explain the dashboard on my 1965 Chevrolet, I told him that the speedometer measures in miles, not kilometers. But it turned out that he was only interested in the total mileage driven, some 82,000 miles. Evidently Russian cars wear out faster and they were astonished that my car was still in such good condition.

In his convention talk, Eremenko reported that Russia's Siberian gas reserves were huge and Russian oil reserves were limited, and they needed to consider other energy sources. Noting that Russia's largest oil fields were in the Volga Urals, western Siberia, and middle Asia, he said that their engineers had not been able to pipe oil through permafrost, the same obstacle we faced in trying to get oil to the continental United States from the vast oil deposits in Alaska. Eremenko's talk was not well received because of his strong accent and the poor quality of his slides.

I began sizing up the Russians. I thought many of Eremenko's claims were exaggerated, and I concluded that the U.S. was far ahead of Russia in oil research. I also surmised from my conversations with

Ovanesov that he wasn't a geologist but probably a KGB or similar type of government agent.

When the convention ended, the Russians gave me two gifts in gratitude for my hospitality—a wooden carving of a horse-drawn carriage and a record of classical music by Russian composers that included a Shostakovich symphony. When I drove them to the airport for their return flight, I was pleased that our astronauts had returned home safely and the convention had ended successfully, notwithstanding my doubts about the Russians.

A FURTHER INTRODUCTION TO OIL DEPOSITS

One of the most basic laws that forms the foundation for geologic science and is the most misunderstood and unfathomable to many people is that of geologic time. Many rocks occur in layers thousands of feet thick and extend laterally for hundreds of miles, either buried deeply or exposed on the earth's surface. They can be hundreds of millions of years old. James Hutton (1726-1797) was the first geologist to recognize the immensity of geologic time. Prior theory posited that the earth was only a few thousand years old. By correctly interpreting the exposed rocks at Siccar Point, UK, near Edinburgh as an angular unconformity, he determined the earth to be millions of years old.

From fossils and the rocks' physical characteristics, geologists decipher their mode of deposition: in an ocean deep or the shallow near-shore, in rivers, lakes, swamps, on land as sand dunes, from volcanic activity, or in many other settings. Minerals found in

Siccar Point, Scotland, showing angular unconformity leading to Hutton's discovery.

rocks—such as the hydrocarbons (oil, gas), coal, uranium, precious metals (gold, silver), industrial minerals (iron, copper, lead, etc.)—fuel the world's economy and drive mankind, conditioned only by economic and environmental issues.

In addition to conventional oil and gas fields, commercial oil occurs in three other types of deposits: 1) as tar sands, a large contributor to the world's oil supply; 2) as shale oil, only recently developed as the result of new horizontal-drilling technology, and 3) as oil shale, long known for its potential but also its economic problems.

To the oil industry, the word "Athabasca"[xiii] signifies huge oil reserves, such as those of Saudi Arabia. The Athabasca tar sands are huge deposits of unconsolidated sand impregnated with bitumen or heavy crude oil located in northeastern Alberta, Canada, about 525 miles north of the U.S. international boundary bordering Montana (plate I). These deposits cover an area of about 54,000 square miles, a little more than half of the size of the state of Colorado. They contain

A FURTHER INTRODUCTION TO OIL DEPOSITS

about 1.7 trillion barrels of bitumen in place, which is comparable to the world's total proven conventional oil reserves. Recoverable oil, depending on price, is estimated at 170 billion barrels, making Canada's Athabasca recoverable reserves one of the largest in the world. Recovery method is by mining operations (plate II) or in-situ technology. Current daily production is about one million barrels, with an expected increase to more than three million barrels by 2020.

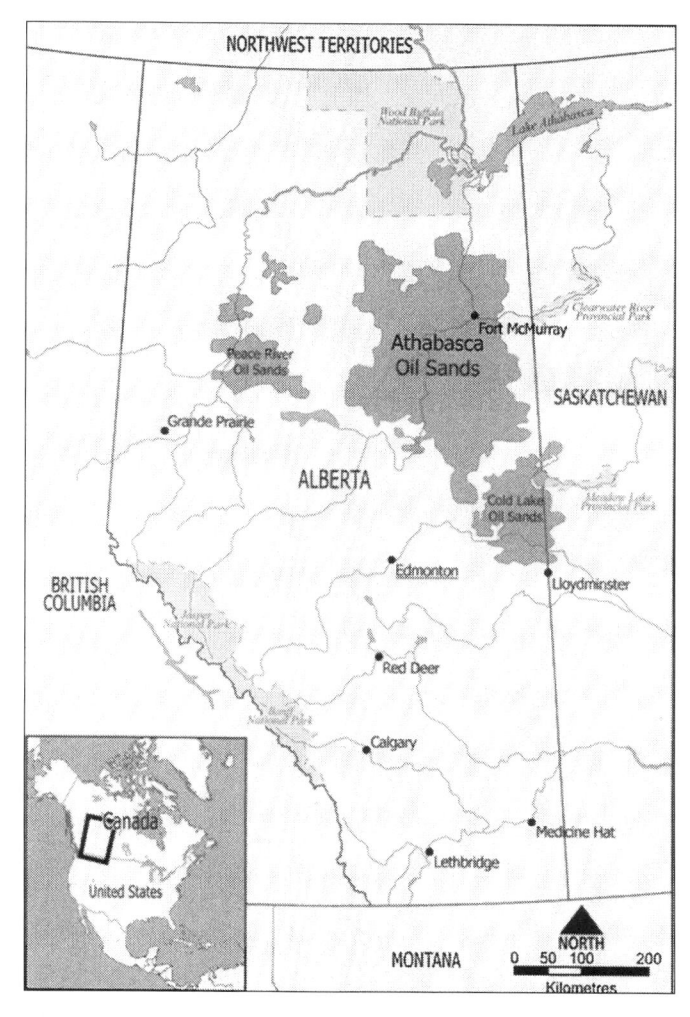

Plate I. Location of Athabasca oil-impregnated sands.

Plate II. Mining operations, Athabasca (courtesy of Shell).

Enormous deposits of oil-impregnated sandstone also occur in northeastern Utah at Sunnyside and Asphalt Ridge but they have not reached Athabasca's level of development.

Unlike the clearly labeled tar sands, shale oil and oil shale might appear to be synonymous but actually are vastly different for the purposes of oil exploration and development.

Shale is a very fine-grained sedimentary rock composed of clays and silt-sized particles. Some of these shales contain significant amounts of organic matter from the microscopic remains of tiny plants and animals. These include plants such as algae, spores, and pollen and animals such as foraminifera, radiolaria, coccoliths, and a number of others. In some settings, these microscopic organisms are deposited by the hundreds of billions, resulting in shales containing 5% to 10% organic matter by volume. This organic matter is called kerogen, defined as any fossilized organic matter that is not soluble in water.

A FURTHER INTRODUCTION TO OIL DEPOSITS

Natural heat and pressure of the earth converts kerogen to oil or gas when kerogen-bearing shales are buried deep enough and long enough (i.e., for millions of years). These are shale oils (or shale gases). The Bakken is a shale oil, one of the richest in the U.S.

Oil shales are different. The most important oil shales in the U.S., in western Colorado and northeastern Utah, contain lots of kerogen but are exposed at the surface or occur at shallow depths. Because they were never buried deeply enough and long enough in the earth, they have not generated hydrocarbons. These oil shales should more properly be called kerogen shales. The reserves of these oil shales are enormous, almost beyond belief, at more than one trillion barrels. But the problem of an economical recovery method has plagued the oil industry.[xiv]

By contrast, shale oils, such as the Bakken, contain clean, easily refinable oil. A piece of Bakken shale weighing ten pounds will yield 1.2 pounds of refinable crude oil. This is expressed in geochemistry terms as the TOC (total organic carbon) of the shale (12% in this example). These shales were deposited in marine (ocean) or lacustrine (lake) environments and have been buried for millions of years deep in the earth's crust. Shales that reach the oil-generating stage are called mature shales. Immature shales, such as oil shales, have not reached the oil-generating stage.

When mature shales, rich in kerogen, convert to hydrocarbons in the earth, an increase in volume occurs (as water does when it freezes) and over-pressuring results. This causes fracturing, making it into a fractured reservoir, but not always a high-quality one. For example, a vertically drilled well can expose a twenty-foot-thick, fractured reservoir to the well bore; however, these wells still might not be commercially productive because of the reservoir's initial poor quality. Fortunately, a new technology has been developed that has revolutionized oil and gas exploration in shale reservoirs: horizontal drilling. Instead of twenty feet exposed to the well bore, horizontal drilling exposes 5,000 to 15,000 feet of the reservoir to the well bore (see plates III and IV). Well bores less than six inches in diameter can be drilled and steered horizontally in a targeted layer of rock (even one that is only ten to twenty feet thick), as far as 15,000 feet. This amazing technology dramatically increases the number of fractures encountered and the recoverable reserves of oil and gas.

Additional fractures are created by a process called hydraulic fracturing.[xv] A mixture of water and sand is pumped down a well under very high pressure and enters the reservoir. It enlarges the existing fractures and also causes additional new fracturing. The sand also acts as a proppant to keep the fractures open and allows oil to flow more freely to the well bore.

The Bakken Shale reservoir in Elm Coulee Field in eastern Montana and the Bakken Shale reservoir in Parshall Field, North Dakota, were two of the first successful, horizontally-drilled oil and gas fields in the U.S. Using these as models or analogs, scores of new projects have emerged throughout the country, as well as in Europe and Asia. It is this new technology that could help bring us oil independence—which leads to another important topic, oil and gas price history and U.S. energy policy.

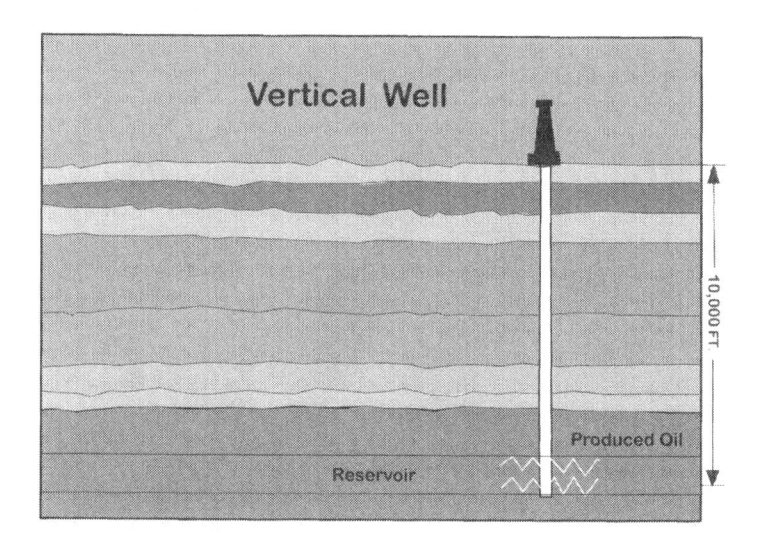

Plate III. Oil recovery from a vertical well.

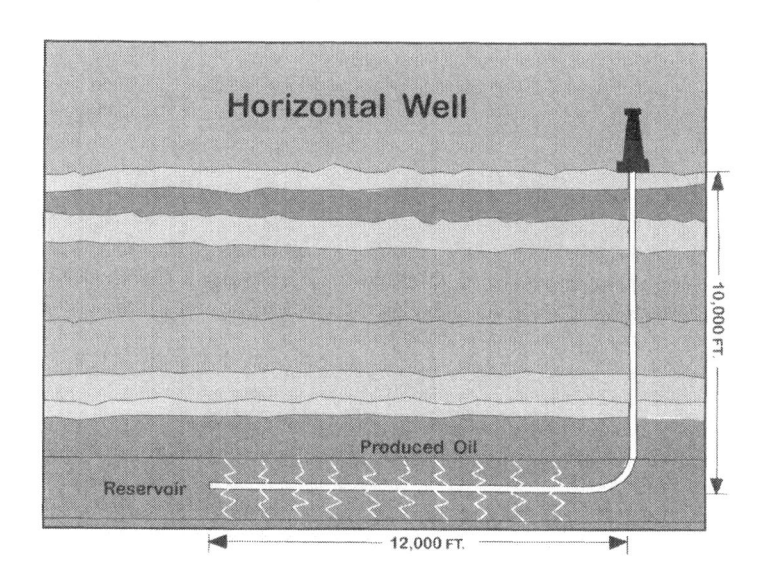

Plate IV. Oil recovery from a horizontal well.

OIL-GAS PRICE HISTORY AND UNITED STATES ENERGY POLICY

In the 1930s, surplus U.S. oil production had driven oil price downward from one or two dollars per barrel to as low as ten cents per barrel. To encourage production, the federal government even attempted to put a floor on oil price. In the 1920s, as an incentive, the depletion allowance had been passed that allowed 27.5% (later reduced to 15%) of oil production to be free of tax.

During World War II and for the next twenty-eight years, oil remained at under five dollars per barrel. The Six-Day War of 1967 had little effect on U.S. demand because new domestic oil discoveries supplied the growing domestic market.

However, the Yom Kippur War in October 1973 caused the first dramatic rise in oil price. When the U.S. sided with Israel in the conflict, the OPEC powerhouses (Iran, Iraq and Saudi Arabia) placed an oil embargo on the U.S. Oil price shot up to fourteen dollars per barrel. It would be the first time that the world would be confronted

THE PRAIRIE OIL & GAS COMPANY

INDEPENDENCE, KANSAS
JULY 13, 1931

NOTICE

Effective 7:00 A.M. July 9, 1931, we will pay the following prices for crude oil purchased in Kansas, Oklahoma and Texas.

Below 29 degrees gravity	.10
29 - 29.9 " "	.11
30 - 30.9 " "	.12
31 - 31.9 " "	.13
32 - 32.9 " "	.14
33 - 33.9 " "	.15
34 - 34.9 " "	.16
35 - 35.9 " "	.17
36 - 36.9 " "	.18
37 - 37.9 " "	.19
38 - 38.9 " "	.20
39 - 39.9 " "	.21
40 degrees and above	.22

Ten barrels of oil for one dollar!

with reality and recognize that oil is a world commodity and oil price is affected by geopolitical issues. By 1980, due to the Shah's overthrow in Iran and the ensuing Iranian political revolution, followed by the Iran-Iraq War, oil rose to the then-unimaginable price of almost forty dollars per barrel. For the next twenty-three years, until 2003, OPEC was able to manipulate the oil price, because they controlled 30% of world oil supply. In a quirk of nature, the Middle East occupies less than 5% of the earth's surface but has 50% of its oil reserves—and only slightly less of the world's gas reserves. World oil price was dictated by OPEC and varied from a low of eleven dollars to thirty dollars per barrel, except during the Gulf War in 1991 when it peaked above the thirty-dollar level. I very vividly remember the low oil price reached in the summer of 1986. Saudi Arabia announced that they would no longer solely take up the slack when Saudi Arabia's OPEC partners were cheating on their export quotas. A price war begun by the Saudis fighting for their fair quota share resulted in the oil price plummeting to eleven dollars per barrel. I owned an interest in a small North Dakota oil producer making only ten barrels of oil per day and also producing fifty barrels of water per day. Water disposal costs exceeded the oil income. In July, OPEC partners settled their differences and the price rose again to the 25-to-30-dollar level. From 2003 to 2014, oil had an incredible ride, peaking at 128 dollars per barrel in 2008, dropping to forty dollars per barrel a year later, then going back up to the ninety-dollars-per-barrel range. Major causes of the price variance were the Kuwaiti War, China's rising economy, the Fukushima nuclear disaster and the Middle East powder keg of Israel versus Iran. The world should take note that every day oil tankers loaded with over 17 million barrels of crude oil, headed for European and Asian markets, pass through the Gulf of Hormuz bordering an unpredictable Iran.

In June 2015, oil price began to collapse again, dropping 40% to the 40-to-50-dollars-per-barrel range by December. In North Dakota, oil price dropped from ninety to about thirty dollars per barrel. The price drop had been predicted but not with such severity. It had a devastating effect on oil activity. Active rigs dropped from 1600 to 734. Cause of the price drop was the over-supply created by a two-million-barrel-per-day increase in oil production by the U.S., triggered by the shale oil boom. Saudi Arabia, OPEC's largest producer, could have reduced this world oil-price drop by agreeing to cut their 10-million-barrel-per-day supply of oil to the world market by a like amount, but that was not done. Instead, the Saudis elected to allow the price to drop. Iran was offered the same opportunity but also declined. The Saudis wanted to help China's economy, since that country is a large oil importer of theirs and an important exporter of goods to the Middle East and to cause economic hardship to its adversaries Iran and Russia. Their actions also challenged U.S. shale oil production which, because of high drilling costs, requires a high oil price in order to be produced economically. In response, U.S. oil firms cut drilling and completion costs by employing modern computerized technology. Operators can drill the vertical 9500 foot hole now in only four days and the horizontal lateral in five or six more, thus reducing drilling time by more than half. New frack techniques and doubling sand volume have increased initial flow rates.

Gyrations in oil price undoubtedly will continue. Russia, Venezuela and Nigeria need an oil price of 80 to 90 dollars per barrel in order to balance their budgets. What is certain is that energy demand in the U.S will increase, and oil will be a large part of that increase for the near future. As an example, comparing U.S. oil supply in June 2015 with June 2014, according to *Oil & Gas Journal* figures, domestic production increased, LNG (liquefied natural gas) increased, imported oil decreased and total supply increased from 18,281,000 bopd (barrels of oil per day) to 19,715,000 bopd, mainly from unconventional sources.

Natural gas, the energy of the future, has had a complicated and uneven price history. Prior to the early 1970s, gas was in plentiful supply but lacked large markets and pipeline outlets. It was an unwanted commodity. Some gas was even flared. It sold for less than fifteen cents per mcf (a thousand cubic feet). But by the mid-1970s, the realization that natural gas was cheap and clean led to a sudden demand increase, peaking at a crisis level in the winter of 1976-77. Nationwide gas shortages occurred. Gas legislation dating from the 1930s needed to be amended to stimulate gas production; some new legislation benefited gas producers, leading to gas price increases. In 1979, gas price rose to one dollar per mcf (wellhead price) and by 1985 increased to $2.50 per mcf. From then until 2000, gas price was steady at $1.50 to $2.25 per mcf. Gas shortages were balanced by new gas reserves, found in the deep offshore of the Gulf of Mexico in the mid-continent, and by importing gas by the building of LNG plants, a new factor. The decade from 2000 to 2010 saw a dramatic increase in demand, resulting in price peaks at over $10.00 per mcf.

In the early 2000s, with the new horizontal-drilling technology breakthrough, the U.S. became flooded with new gas reserves. The Marcellus Shale gas reservoir present over large parts of Pennsylvania, West Virginia, New York, Maryland, and Virginia, millions of acres in size, has the potential of satisfying gas demand in the northeastern U.S. markets for 100 years.

The Barnett Shale gas reservoir in the Fort Worth, Texas area is where fracking for shale gas was pioneered. George Mitchell, owner of Mitchell Energy, spent more than ten years perfecting frack treatments that turned the Barnett into a major gas field with reserves exceeding 33 trillion cubic feet of gas and 120 million barrels of oil. He was rewarded for his efforts in 2013 when Mitchell Energy was sold to Devon for 2.3 billion dollars.

The Haynesville gas reservoir in east Texas and northwestern Louisiana, the Fayetteville in northern Arkansas, and the Utica Shale in eastern Ohio and western Pennsylvania are other recently discovered gas reservoirs that have developed into major size gas fields. Newly discovered gas reserves in the U.S., based on The Potential Gas Committee and the EIA (U.S. Energy Information Administration) figures, total an amazing 2515 trillion cubic feet! Natural gas is the shining star as the energy of the future and the U.S. is awash in it. Because of this massive over-supply, recent gas price has been low, in the $2.25-to-$2.75-per-mcf range, and development has slowed. It should be noted that nearly all of these new gas discoveries were not made by the majors but by independent U.S. oil companies on state, Indian and fee (private, non-governmental) lands. From a global perspective, this is particularly noteworthy, since the U.S. is the only country in the world where mineral interests are owned by non-federal entities.[xvi]

Since the Carter administration (1977-1981), the U.S. has attempted to establish a positive national energy policy in order to increase domestic oil production. However, some governmental legislation has even restrained oil development, such as the Crude Oil Windfall Profit Tax passed in 1980. It was not a tax on profits, but an excise tax on most of the oil produced. As a result, domestic oil production declined, imports increased and oil prices hit new lows. By 1988, the tax was repealed.

Positive steps in energy policy have ranged from "turning off the lights" to increasing the efficiencies of lighting and appliances. Federal and state tax credits were established as incentives for improving insulation in homes and other buildings. In the future solar panels will be used for household operations, as solar energy gains popularity.

During the early 1980s, the U.S. Petroleum Reserve was established; by June 2012, it held some 695 million barrels of oil to be used for emergency needs. These oil reserves are stored in huge salt caverns in Louisiana along the coastline of the Gulf of Mexico. They are a significant deterrent to oil import cutoffs.

Coal, our cheapest energy source, rose in use from 697 million tons in 1977 to a record amount of slightly more than a billion tons in 1990 and remained at that level until 2011. However, the average share of electrical generation from coal in the U.S. dropped from 52% to 45% in 2010 and then to 39% by 2013. Usage will continue to drop due to industries switching to natural gas and the Environmental Protection Agency's plan to regulate greenhouse-gas emissions.

Another U.S. energy resource is nuclear power. Currently, ninety-nine commercial nuclear reactors generate approximately 20% of our total electrical energy. The U.S. has adopted very strict nuclear energy safety standards as a result of the 1979 accident at the Three Mile Island nuclear plant in Pennsylvania. Due to the government's close scrutiny of the industry and high plant-infrastructure costs, no new nuclear plants have been built for twenty years, although there is a great deal of renewed interest.

Renewable energy sources such as solar, wind, and geothermal, plus cars powered by electricity, energy hybrids, batteries, and new combustion engines with higher quality gasoline, will compete in the market place in ever-changing incarnations that will become cheaper to buy and more efficient to use. This transformation will require more than twenty-five years to become meaningful. Oil and gas will be the essential bridge to this transformed future because of their versatile uses and current role in maintaining the lifestyle to which we are accustomed.

To meet these bridging needs, more federal offshore oil and gas leases need to be made available in the Gulf of Mexico, in order to develop new oil and gas fields. The oil and gas reserves in this area account for 25% of total domestic production. Forty percent of the U.S. petroleum refining capacity is also located there. The Gulf of Mexico has become an experimental area and a proving ground for development of new offshore technology that is spreading to other parts of the U.S. and to the world. Shell's Perdido Spar, with three oil fields, is being developed in 8000 feet of water 100 miles offshore from Texas. Two more of the many, deep offshore fields, BHP Billiton's Shenzi field in 4400 feet of water, and BP's Atlantis Field in 6100 feet of water (both producing from Miocene-age rocks) demonstrate the advance in drilling technology being used to develop the huge oil and gas reserves of the deeper portion of the Gulf of Mexico. The potential is unprecedented. In addition, we need to expand federal offshore leasing along the eastern U.S. coast and Alaska. New oil and gas discoveries in these areas could fill existing pipelines not currently transporting hydrocarbons at full capacity.

A second way to address energy security is by expanding and developing our unconventional oil and gas resources to include those on federal lands. To date, the new petroleum technologies have been able to play a key role only because they have been utilized on non-federal lands only. Strict—and, in some cases, prohibitive—regulations have rendered federal lands unusable.

Horizontal drilling and new reservoir-stimulation technologies (fracking) have completely revolutionized oil and gas exploration in the U.S. In the last nine years, this technology has led to independent oil companies discovering nearly all of the billions of barrels of new oil reserves, thus significantly reducing our oil imports. At Parshall, the leading operators have been EOG Resources, Inc.; Whiting Petroleum Corporation; Slawson Exploration Company, Inc.; Continental Resources, Inc.; Oasis Petroleum, Inc.; Hess Corporation; Statoil; and Petro-Hunt Oil Company.

In 2006, we imported 65% of our oil. This imported amount has now been reduced to 37%, a 28% reduction that puts hundreds of billions of dollars back into the U.S. economy. Until the price drop in mid-2015, domestic oil production was increasing at a rate of twenty-five to fifty thousand barrels per month. By late 2015, the U.S. became the world's largest oil producer, overtaking Saudi Arabia and Russia—all due to horizontal drilling and new fracking technology.

Governmental approval to construct the Keystone XL Pipeline, vetoed by President Obama in 2015, would further facilitate transporting Athabasca crude oil from Alberta to mid-America and southward to the Gulf Coast, providing more than one million barrels per day of much-needed production.

However, we should handle America's huge energy resources in an environmentally responsible manner. In part, the government has addressed this by creating tax credits (as incentives for insulating heated homes and office buildings) and setting greenhouse-gas performance standards for existing coal-fired power plants. In addition, we should increase safeguards against oil spills, such as BP's Deepwater Horizon spill that dumped 4.9 million barrels into the Gulf of Mexico, and remain vigilant in oversight of nuclear plants.

The surge of drilling in shale reservoirs has caused concerns about their effect on social welfare. Fracking is receiving a great deal of negative publicity, but fracking needs to be viewed scientifically and economically. The first frack job took place in 1947, when

Stanolind used it on a gas well in the huge Hugoton gas field in western Kansas. Since then, hundreds of thousands of frack jobs have been completed in the U.S. Thousands of oil fields in the U.S., including Parshall and Elm Coulee, would not exist today were it not for fracking treatment. Sand and water ordinarily make up 98% of a frack job. In the offing is a new CO_2 frack which would be liquid free. Fracking should be regulated by state agencies, rather than federal ones, and they should bear responsibility for all associated environmental concerns.

FUTURE ENERGY USE
Importance of Fossil Fuels

Future energy use by energy type is a vital topic on which to reflect. In the next twenty-five years, what will happen to oil imports: will they disappear? If you ponder cheap and dirty coal or (everyone's favorite) the renewables, you have to wonder what the percentage of each energy used will be, by type, by the year 2040.

First, U.S. energy use will continue its fifty-year-long increase, partly due to our predicted population increase from 310 to over 325 million. Currently at 52-million-barrels-per-day equivalent (converting all energy types to barrels of oil, at a 1.5% increase yearly), it is slated to increase to 75.5 million barrels per day by 2040. Fossil fuels (oil, natural gas and coal) now make up 83% of total energy use. By 2040, the largest increase will be in renewables, and the largest decrease in coal.

OIL - Oil is the largest and most important energy type at 35% of current total energy use. Gasoline, refined from crude oil, is what

FUTURE U.S. ENERGY USE

	2015 % Energy Use	2015 Share of 52 mmboe/day	2040 % Energy Use	2040 Share of 75.5 mmboe/day
OIL	35%	18.20	30%	22.65
GAS	28%	14.56	32%	24.16
COAL	20%	10.40	12%	9.06
NUCLEAR	9%	4.68	9%	6.795
HYDROELECTRIC	5%	2.60	4%	3.02
RENEWABLES	<u>3%</u>	<u>1.56</u>	<u>13%</u>	<u>9.815</u>
	100%	52 mmboe/day	100%	75.5 mmboe/day

Figure 1. Percentage of use by energy type, in total barrels of oil equivalent per day in 2015 and 2040, showing an increase in total usage of 1.5% per year and based on a current total of 52 mmboe/day. Largest increase is in renewables; largest decrease in coal. Biomass, a renewable, is not included in this figure.

Figure 1. Percentage of use by energy type, in total barrels of oil equivalent per day in 2015 and 2040.

fuels combustion engines running the 260-million U.S. car fleet. Oil also has other uses—in plastics, petrochemicals, road materials, paint, weed killers, antifreeze, candles, dyes, pesticides, pharmaceuticals and hundreds of other products.

Oil usage should peak in the next ten years and then begin a slow downward trend, replaced by cleaner energy types. Oil imports, now 37% of daily consumption, down from 65% only eight years ago, will continue to decline. The last oil imports to disappear, if ever, will be crude imported from Canada (including crude from the Athabasca oil sands which is partly U.S.-owned), plus Mexico and Saudi Arabia (which owns interests in Texas refineries). Domestic production had been increasing at a rate of a half million barrels a year, mainly due to the shale and unconventional drilling boom. Currently, total daily oil consumption is 20.2 million barrels, of which 8.5 million barrels is domestic crude, 3.6 million barrels is LNG and 8.1 million barrels is imported crude oil on long-term contracts to domestic refineries equipped for refining lower-quality imported crude (September 2016 figures, *Oil & Gas Journal*). Self-sufficiency is many years away.

NATURAL GAS - The fossil energy of the future, it is cleaner than oil and much more plentiful. We have more than a 100-year gas supply located near large markets in the Northeast from the Marcellus and Utica shale reservoirs and huge additional gas reserves in the mid-continent. Due to over-supply, development of this asset is hampered by low gas prices. The usage of natural gas as a percent of total fossil fuels will increase yearly because it is a cleaner fuel, destined to replace coal and crude oil. Natural gas currently makes up 28% of total energy use.

COAL - A fossil fuel and the most-polluting energy type, coal is widely used in the U.S. because of its low cost and plentiful supply. We lead the world in coal reserves with over 260 billion tons. It is the dominant fuel for power plants, supplying 39% of the nation's electricity. Because of global warming issues, a united drive to reduce the burning of coal is underway. Most coal-fired power plants will not be able to meet current U.S. emission standards. Switching to natural gas is a more likely scenario than refitting coal-fired power plants, particularly with gas currently at less than three dollars per mcf. Coal will continue to decrease in use, replaced by natural gas or the renewable energies. Coal currently makes up 20% of total U.S. energy use.

NUCLEAR - The future of nuclear power is hard to predict. The sole purpose of a nuclear plant is to generate electricity. Twenty percent of the nation's electricity is produced by the ninety-nine U.S.

nuclear plants, none of which emits any CO_2 or other pollutants. Heat, generated by fission, boils water into steam which is used to turn the turbines that produce electricity. The average age of U.S. commercial nuclear reactors is thirty-four years; the last one was built twenty years ago.

The Three Mile Island incident, in March 1979 in Pennsylvania, cemented anti-nuclear thinking in the U.S., though radiation effects were minimal. In 1986, Russia's devastating Chernobyl incident was blamed for later causing cancer in 4000 children, compounding the difficulty of reversing opposition to nuclear power. This disaster was followed by the unfortunate Fukushima catastrophe, which killed thousands of people. There is no better example of a *force majeure* incident than this. An earthquake-created tsunami on Japan's coast damaged a nuclear plant's water pumps, which were designed to cool the fuel rods. The fuel rods overheated and later caused the deadly explosion, but radiation killed no one.

In spite of all this, nuclear power in the U.S. is enjoying a revival. Four or five nuclear plants in the southeastern U.S. are in the planning stage—all designed in the form of a new, modern, standard model that can be used repeatedly, thus reducing design and construction costs. What nuclear energy offers is round-the-clock electricity during any weather conditions with no CO_2 emissions or air pollution, at stable electricity pricing and without government subsidies or tax credits. However, in the U.S., nuclear faces strong political opposition. China has twenty-five nuclear plants in operation and some twenty-four others are in various stages of completion. India and Russia also have plans to build multiple nuclear reactors. France has surpassed everyone by having adopted nuclear power years ago so that today 75% of its electricity is nuclear-generated.

FUTURE ENERGY USE: IMPORTANCE OF FOSSIL FUELS

Should a triumph of science over politics occur, use of nuclear energy in the U.S. could slowly increase in volume in the future, but the percentage of total energy use will remain at about 9%, due to the overall volume increases in most of the other types of energy.

HYDROELECTRIC - Of the tens of thousands of dams in the U.S., only about 2500 produce hydroelectric power. Hydropower produces only 5% of total U.S. electricity usage. The main use of dams in the U.S. is for irrigation, flood control, water supply and recreational programs. Congress has attempted to subsidize the building of power plants at dam sites but with little success. Very little increase in the percentage of hydroelectrically-generated electricity is contemplated.

RENEWABLES - The energies of the future—wind, solar and geothermal—will increase dramatically in the future but at a slower rate than predicted. Autos powered by electricity, batteries, natural gas, or other renewable combinations will slowly replace a part of the U.S. car fleet of about 260 million vehicles. However, by 2040, only 15 to 20% of the U.S. car fleet will be renewable-energy-powered because it will take years to establish a nationwide refueling system. Tesla, the leading electric car producer, sold only 50,000 robot-assembled, beautifully-designed autos in 2015 at a buyer's cost of over $90,000 (latest model price is 30% lower). Ownership cost of conventional cars will decline. Wind is the largest but solar, although smaller, is the fastest-growing source of renewable energy in America. However, both are intermittent energy sources: the wind does not always blow and the sun does not always shine. They will both need a large grid in order to compete in the marketplace. Hybrid aircraft engines are still only in the early planning stage. Though renewables currently make up only a small percentage of total energy use, they will grow at an exponential rate by 2040 to an estimated 13%.

Very important, all of these predictions assume that no dramatic breakthrough in energy sources will occur, though a model for fusion (i.e., fusing atoms rather than splitting them) has recently been announced by Lockheed.

LATE TWENTIETH-CENTURY ISSUES
Climate Change and World Events

During the last twenty years of the twentieth century, climate change and other environmental issues moved to the forefront of public consciousness. By 1988, climate change was emerging as a major political issue. In November of that year, the Intergovernmental Panel on Climate Change (IPCC) was formed because over 80% of the world's energy was coming from the burning of fossil fuels causing climate change. Discourse on greenhouse gases and global warming was beginning.[xvii]

From the Reagan administration on, emissions and pollutants were increasingly restricted and regulated. Tetraethyl lead, used in gasoline since the 1920s to remove the knock in car engines, was declared damaging to human health and banned in the early 1980s. In 1980, the term "acid rain" was coined to describe the sulfur dioxide (SO_2) from coal-burning power plants reacting in the atmosphere to form sulfuric and nitric acids, which are damaging to forests, lakes, and sea life. By 2008, SO_2 emissions decreased by 60% from 1980 levels, largely due to an emission trading system.[xviii]

New warnings and constraints have continued to hit the headlines virtually every year. In 1987, the Montreal Protocol restricted the use of chlorofluorocarbons believed to be causing damage to the ozone layer in Antarctica.[xix] In 1990 the IPCC was readying its first report for the United Nations General Assembly, warning that the earth was warming; whether the cause was anthropogenic (burning of fossil fuels) or due to natural climate variables (the sun, oceans, the El Niño effect, earth's heat, as well as cyclic climate history) is still being debated.

An observable example of cyclic climate history is found in reviewing the glacial history of North America. For about a million years, ending only 12,000 years ago, glaciers hundreds of feet high occupied parts of the northern U.S. The glaciers eroded deeply into the Earth and their melted remnants formed the Great Lakes (Superior, Michigan, Huron, Erie and Ontario), 95,000 square miles in area, the largest body of fresh water in the world perhaps with the exception of Lake Baikal in Siberia. Moraines are topographic features, hills and ridges made up of till (unstratified and unconsolidated debris) hundreds of feet thick, transported and deposited by glaciers. Frontal moraines occur at the front edge of a glacier that is at a standstill and where huge amounts of till are dumped. Over periods of thousands of years, glaciers have advanced (indicating colder climate) and retreated (indicative of warmer climate) and their front margins are marked by frontal moraines. They are easily seen in the northern Great Plains of the middle and western United States. Glaciers are an outstanding example of natural climate change.

The real climate problem lies in China and India. They account for over 30% of the world's greenhouse gas emissions and, even worse, in the next several years their percentage will increase, not decrease. The U.S. has decreased greenhouse gas emissions in the last few years and the emerging countries need to follow our example. Meanwhile, with a carbon tax, gasoline currently sells for seven dollars a gallon in London and Paris (as high as twelve dollars last year) and for less than three dollars in the U.S. The reasons for the lower price here are the oil over-supply, this climate debate and the adverse effect that higher gasoline prices would have on our economy.

In the 1990s, meetings involving thousands of people from all parts of the world were held to determine how to deal with the burning of fossil fuels. On June 3rd, 1992, the Rio Accord talks, attended by over 10,000 people, were convened by the U.N. to form an agreement limiting greenhouse gas emissions. The European nations wanted timetables for reducing emissions, but the U.S. balked, and the talks would end with an agreement of limited scope.[xx] The Kyoto Accord talks, held in Japan in 1997, were another attempt to set binding targets for greenhouse gas emissions and how to implement them. What emerged was an agreement, not a treaty, which reduced emissions and also provided for a market trading system.[xxi]

Three more conferences were held over the next six years. The one held in Copenhagen in 2009 nearly collapsed but was salvaged with adoption of a weak non-binding statement. The next climate conference was held in Warsaw in November 2013; it served to prepare nations for a universal agreement to be ratified at the Paris Conference to be held in 2015. Following it was the climate conference held in Lima, Peru. Concluded in November 2014, it was an attempt to get all nations involved in cutting greenhouse gas emissions but was not supported by the poorer nations.[xxii]

The Paris Climate Conference, concluded in December 2015 and attended by 195 countries, set as a goal limiting the rise in the earth's temperature to 1.5°C above pre-industrial levels. That goal was not achieved. The conference recognized that they would not be able to force poor, emerging countries to reduce their use of fossil fuels because they are so necessary to their economies. The Paris Conference offered new ideas, however, for future reduction of greenhouse gases. One solution was to require the developed, rich countries to subsidize the poor countries' costs in adapting to the effects of climate change. China, the world's largest emitter, indicated that it would lower its percentage of increase in greenhouse gas emissions. Though the U.S. has already set the global example by lowering emissions starting a few years ago, it pledged further decreases. A future climate conference is planned for 2018.

Two major world events in the early 1990s greatly accelerated the threat to control of world oil reserves. The Gulf War began in August 1990 when Iraq invaded Kuwait and took control of its government and valuable oil reserves. It ended in January 1991 as a result of Operation Desert Storm, an effort by a multi-nation coalition led by President George H.W. Bush. Operation Desert Storm restored Kuwait's independence, removing the danger of Middle East oil reserves falling into enemy hands.

Surprisingly, in December 1991, Soviet president Mikhail Gorbachev announced the collapse of the Soviet Union—the end of communism in the land where it started. Because oil and gas income had sustained the economy for years, falling oil prices drastically cut the U.S.S.R.'s revenues: the country could no longer finance the national food supply, the arms race, and needed imports of consumer goods and equipment. It was no longer a super power and was divided into fifteen separate states, with Russia the most powerful.

FAMILY LIFE
A New Stage Unfolds

Well before the U.S.S.R. dissolved, our family was thriving. Using some of the money we had banked from the sale of our interest in South Bishop Ranch oil field, we bought a town lot in a fashionable neighborhood in Littleton, a suburb of Denver. After a trip to Williamsburg to study the Georgian architectural style, we sold our tract house and in 1977 built a Georgian-style home at 1485 Crestridge Drive in Littleton. Years later, in 1989, after Alicia and Mark started living independently, we sold our home and moved to a 350-condo complex in Denver where we still reside.

A particularly enjoyable family trip in 2009 to Greece started in Athens at the Grande Bretagne Hotel. After being shaken by two earthquakes in Santorini, we relaxed during a pleasant visit to Ea, a small town on the corner of the island. From there we traveled by hydrofoil to Crete to delve into the Minoan culture.

Family at Ea, Santorini Island, Greece, 2009.

The highlight of all our travels was our visit in April 2008 with my cousin Evan Poulos and his lovely wife Ann in Johannesburg, South Africa. We were fortunate to be guests at their luxurious home, including a swimming pool, tennis courts, and beautiful gardens, on grounds encompassing several acres. We found Evan and Ann to be warm, hospitable and friendly. Some of the best times we shared with them were chats in their kitchen over coffee. Also, we had the unforgettable experience of going on safari with them. In an armed and armored jeep with a driver-guide and a lookout sitting on the front left fender, we rode for four days through Ngala, an upscale game reserve near the coast of the Indian Ocean. We saw all of "the big five"—water buffalos, lions, rhinos, hippos, and elephants (some in herds)—as well as giraffes and other animals. Once we parked the jeep for fifteen minutes in dead silence in the bush; from only fifteen yards away, we watched a leopard family with three six-week-old cubs. It was truly a memorable experience.

FAMILY LIFE: A NEW STAGE UNFOLDS

Elephants grazing in the bush at Ngala Private Game Reserve, South Africa, 2008.

Relaxing in the bush, Ngala, 2008.

We also visited Evan's sister Marina Poulos Hestenes, an oncologist, and her family. A very benevolent person, she has devoted most of her professional career to treating indigent cancer patients, since South Africa does not provide adequate medical care for its citizens.

Tragically, in 2013, Evan was diagnosed with cancer and died in June that year. He died at the peak of his career, greatly admired by all. I lost my closest relative, and his death has had a lasting effect on me—especially when I reflect on the fact that I am twenty-five years his elder. Some of us live a long, full life with success and happiness, a few die young from disease or accidents, and then there are those such as Evan who live a shortened life, when he could have contributed so much more to his loving family and friends.

NORTH DAKOTA
Early Energy Powerhouse

Before the discovery of oil in North Dakota in 1951, several exploration efforts were launched. A major story begins in 1937 with the drilling of the No.1 Kamp well by The California Company (Chevron). It was the first deep well drilled on the Nesson Anticline. It bottomed at a depth of 10,281 feet in the Devonian section. The Schlumberger log run on this well was the first for the state of North Dakota. Formation tops printed on the log include Kinderhook, a U.S. Midwestern geological term equivalent to and predating the Bakken name, which did not appear until 1953. Forty-five short cores were taken, beginning in the Cretaceous and including one across the main Nesson pay zone. However, The California Company lost the opportunity to make the Nesson Anticline oil discovery because only a small portion of that core was recovered. Today, the Kamp well is offset by Nesson pay zone producers.

The Amerada Iverson discovery was completed sixteen years later seven miles northeast of the Kamp well. According to Clay Murray (Amerada's land manager in Tulsa), geologist E.H. McCullough was a member of the geophysical crew that conducted the seismic survey for The California Company in the mid-1930s prior to the drilling of their well. He later rose to become president of Amerada and, remembering the history of the Kamp well, leased the Nesson Anticline acreage—for only ten cents per acre! The Iverson discovery well missed all of the shallower pay zones and was completed in the Silurian Interlake dolomite at a depth of 11,630 feet.

Some of the later highlights in North Dakota's oil exploration history include:

1. Development by Amerada and others of the huge Nesson Anticline oil fields, with reserves exceeding 500 million barrels.
2. Later, in the 1950s, discovery of oil in the shallower east portion of the Williston Basin, which opened the entire west half of the state of North Dakota to oil exploration.
3. The recognition of limestone and dolomite as important reservoirs and of the extremely important fracture and microfracture type of porosity—all of which were literally unknown heretofore in the Rockies. This was quickly followed by discovery of carbonate stratigraphic-type traps, which now make up a large portion of North Dakota's oil reserves.
4. Incidents of casing destruction caused by the mobile nature of salt layers in the subsurface, hundreds of feet thick in the Charles formation—a problem that led to the enormously costly re-drilling of hundreds of wells, later solved by the introduction of salt-based drilling mud.

5. Discovery of Antelope (1953) and Elkhorn Ranch (1961) oil fields, the first two significant Bakken reservoir fields.
6. In 1967, an extensive, shallow Cretaceous exploration program in the Williston Basin (although that initial effort failed, probably due to lack of thermally-mature source rocks), after the discovery of Bell Creek Field (Muddy Sandstone reservoir) in Montana—a 133-million-barrel oil field.
7. Discovery in 1977 of Little Knife Field, with produced reserves of 93 million barrels mainly from the Madison and Bakken reservoirs, which led to the discovery of numerous other fields on the Billings Nose, a very low-relief structural feature.
8. Introduction in 1987 of horizontal drilling, spurred by new tax incentives, which led to the drilling of a large number of horizontally drilled Upper Bakken Shale wells in Elkhorn Ranch and in the Billings Nose fields, most of which were marginally commercial.
9. Discovery of unusual oil traps, originating from meteor-impact craters, at Red Wing Creek (with reserves of 60 million barrels) and Newporte fields.
10. Launching of the Lodgepole (Waulsortian-type mound) play in Stark County in 1995—an effort based on excellent reserves (the three-well Dickinson field has produced over 12 million barrels), but ultimately revealing, after an extensive search covering millions of acres extending even into Canada and at a cost of several hundred million dollars, a very tiny areal extent.[xxiii]

11. The limited success of a horizontally-drilled program in the shallow Madison Limestone reservoir in the Nesson Anticline fields, due to lack of horizontal-drilling and fracking technology.
12. In the 1990s, development of the first significant, horizontally-drilled, commercial oil field in North Dakota—the Cedar Hills Field, in Bowman County in the southwestern corner of the state, from the deep Red River "B" reservoir, with produced reserves of 155 million barrels and total reserves exceeding 250 million barrels.

Despite the significance of these events, what was about to happen in North Dakota not only surpassed these milestones but would astound the oil industry. It would mark a change in oil and gas exploration comparable to the economic change heralded by microchips in the 1960s becoming the heartbeat of the modern world and by IBM's introduction of computers in 1981.

PARSHALL FIELD

A Career Turning-Point

Although our family was enjoying life, oil prices were low and industry activity had slowed down during the 1990s. But suddenly circumstances changed that would transform my professional life forever. It was a moment when perseverance, timing and good fortune all meshed to create a career triumph.

In early 2003, President George W. Bush was still coping with the aftermath of 9/11. New York was recovering from the worst attack by an enemy since Pearl Harbor. Intelligence sources were reporting that Iran would probably lack the capacity to produce enough enriched uranium for a bomb until 2010 or 2015. Fortunately, the economy was thriving. And George Mitchell, of Houston-based Mitchell Energy, was pioneering new fracking technology in the Barnett Shale reservoir in the Fort Worth, Texas area.

At the same time, an unnamed oil field in Richland County, Montana was being explored, targeting the Bakken Shale reservoir at depths of 9000 feet. Operators were small companies like Lyco Energy of Dallas, Continental Resources in Enid, Oklahoma, EOG Resources and Slawson Exploration in Denver, as well as Headington Oil Company owned by my longtime friends (now based in Dallas). The basis for this activity was some non-commercial Bakken oil recoveries from several Bakken wells drilled many years previously. Operators now were trying to perfect a horizontal drilling technique to determine if it would yield commercially viable recoveries from the Bakken reservoir.

From published data, dating back to the 1980s, it was well known that hundreds of billions of barrels of high-gravity oil had been generated in the Bakken Shale, deeply buried in the Williston Basin of Montana and North Dakota (technically, "oil in place"). Though the oil industry had become aware of this enormous potential oil source, what was needed was an engineering breakthrough to find an economical recovery method. Horizontal drilling was emerging as the answer.

It is important to note that, despite the early success in horizontal drilling in southwest North Dakota's Cedar Hills Field, that particular reservoir, the Red River Dolomite, shed limited light on how to use horizontal drilling in the much more elusive Bakken reservoir, because Cedar Hills' reservoir yielded so readily to horizontal drilling. Even though it was 3400 feet deeper than the Bakken, the Cedar Hills reservoir was only five to ten feet thick and sandwiched between two very hard rock layers. The bit stayed in the reservoir layer with little difficulty because it followed the path of least resistance, the thin reservoir layer.

In April 2003, Walter Arbuckle, owner of Denver-based Fossil Associates, called me. He had learned that Lyco Energy was successfully completing horizontally drilled Bakken wells in Richland County's unnamed oil field. Drilling activity was increasing and a large lease play was under way.

Arbuckle was an old friend. We had gone down the Grand Canyon together on a week-long river trip in 1969, and I had fond memories of that adventure. I had a long-standing friendship with him and also knew his partner Elliott Riggs (now deceased), who spent World War II in London at Bletchley Park, working on breaking the Abwehr wireless code and deciphering the German Enigma machine. In 2008, Arbuckle and Riggs were awarded the prestigious Explorer of the Year Award by the Rocky Mountain Association of Geologists (RMAG) for their successes in the Paradox Basin of southwest Colorado. Arbuckle was always interested in financing good geologic prospects. In this case, it was his idea, but he needed help in getting it started.

He asked me if I would be interested in joining a technical team to explore the idea of making a land-lease play in this Montana oil field area. What he wanted from me was a geologic model of the field, soon to be named Elm Coulee: which way would it extend, if any, so that we could lease the oil and gas rights ahead of the drilling activity? Arbuckle arranged for his close friend Sigmund Rosenfeld to do the land work. Andy Logan, a young aggressive engineer, would advise on the project's economics and engineering. Arbuckle would finance the venture, and, in exchange for our work, the three of us would earn an interest in any leasehold obtained.

Denver Earth Resources Library (DERL), capably managed by Kay Waller, has the most complete records of well data in the Rocky Mountain region, so it was there that I collected all of the geologic and engineering data available on this area. Most of the data was in hard-paper copies but some was accessible only on microfiche, which was very time-consuming to research. When I completed my study, I concluded that the field would extend westward. Rosenfeld sent out over 400 offers to landowners and we succeeded in buying only four small tracts within my projected trend. This amounted to only a one-percent success ratio. Soon afterwards, the field made the headlines, lease prices soared, and we were unable to lease any more lands. Our project ended, but, later, all four of these small tracts produced commercially.

Development of Elm Coulee Field progressed rapidly. The pay zone is a sandy dolomite only ten to twenty feet thick with poor reservoir quality. Horizontal drilling and fracking are mandatory for a reservoir of this type, because vertically drilled wells do not expose enough of its low-quality reservoir to the well bore to be commercially productive.

Thanks to the advanced technology of horizontal drilling, Elm Coulee (including Elm Coulee NE) is now more than sixty miles long, with 1130 completed horizontal wells. Daily production for 2014 averaged 50,400 barrels. It is one of Montana's largest oil fields: total recoverable reserves are estimated at over 300 million barrels. By all classifications, it is a major oil field, and it exists solely because of horizontal drilling and fracking technology.

Recognizing the enormous potential of the Bakken reservoir, and the importance of the technological breakthrough of horizontal drilling, I began searching independently for another geologic setting similar to the one at Elm Coulee. My exploration strategy included classifying different areas in the Williston Basin by their potential oil value. An area that has been producing oil and gas for more than twenty years, using oil-finding techniques that are well known, is what I called an "old area." Not much is left to find and what is left is actively being sought by established operators. So you might want to try a "new oil-finding technique" in an old area. Even better, you might try the old area's oil-finding technique in a "new area." Best of all, however, would be using a "new oil-finding technique in a new area." That was my goal. The new oil-finding technique was horizontal drilling—only recently perfected but becoming rapidly recognized for its potential. What I was looking for was a new area that fit the Elm Coulee Field geologic model, but with lands still unleased.

In oil and gas exploration of frontier areas, all of the major disciplines of geology need to be evaluated--geology, geophysics, petroleum engineering and especially geochemistry. There were several basic geologic characteristics of the Bakken in western North Dakota that needed to be closely checked and assessed.

Overall, the Bakken Formation is only about 85 feet thick and subdivided into three members. The upper member consists of black shale, the middle member is the reservoir, consisting mostly of carbonates and sandstone, and the lower member is another black shale. The shales are highly organic, categorized as Type 2 (algal), and deposited in a deep-water-marine, anoxic, low sedimentation-rate setting. TOC is a measure of the organic carbon in a rock and is expressed in its percentage of weight. Bakken TOC values are spectacular, up to 20%; since the average TOC is 12%, Bakken shales rank as one of the richest oil source rocks in the U.S. Hundreds of billions of barrels of oil have been generated by the Bakken in the Williston Basin. Oil is 42 degrees gravity. This oil generation has occurred at a low thermal maturity of 420-430°C Tmax (temperature data from source rock analysis used to indicate thermal maturity), producing hydrocarbons of high quality. It also has volumetrically pressured the rock matrix and generated super-lithostatic pore pressure, causing fracturing of the reservoir. Fracturing is the main porosity type. These issues are more fully explained in a published article that I co-authored with three Bakken experts: Dan Jarvie, Robert Coskey, and Jay Leonard.[xxiv]

My search began a few miles east of Elm Coulee, near the Montana–North Dakota border, and extended fifty miles eastward. For the next few months, using the DERL as my primary information source, I reviewed more than 100 wells located within those fifty miles that had penetrated the Bakken zone. I copied and analyzed well reports and logs—that is, surveys recording electrical, acoustical, neutron-density, gamma-ray intensity and other geophysical characteristics of well bores. Few wells had actually tested the Bakken reservoir; none was significant. Nothing fit my model.

I needed another area to explore, but it wasn't going to be easy to find, since the Nesson Anticline oil fields were immediately to the east of this first search area. This north-south trending series of oil fields—sixty miles long and five to ten miles wide—had been discovered in 1951 by Amerada Petroleum Corporation (now Hess), my first employer. I avoided this area because leases on lands where producing wells are located do not expire. Even if a small leasehold had been available, it would have required a complex and costly land-title search and a high leasing cost. Not surprisingly, reserves of these huge fields now exceed 500 million barrels.

The next area eastward would be the last potential area in my search because its eastern margin was also the eastern margin of mature Bakken Shale. The Williston Basin, a huge bowl-shaped sedimentary basin, extends across all of western North Dakota and parts of Montana, South Dakota, Saskatchewan and Manitoba. Its deepest part is several miles west of the Nesson Anticline, where the Bakken Shale is buried to a depth of 10,500 feet. It shallows eastward so that in a distance of forty-five miles, it is only 8500 feet deep. At this depth, the Bakken Shale becomes immature, meaning that the lithostatic pressure (the weight of the overlying rocks) and the earth's temperature have decreased to a point that oil is not generated.

After eliminating acreage where there was little or no well data, I was left with an area thirty by forty miles square, some 1200 square miles or about 768,000 acres. In this area there were only twenty-five Bakken penetrations, averaging about one well for every 31,000 acres. However, among them was one well drilled in 1997 that had recovered 34,000 barrels of oil from the Bakken reservoir from a short horizontal lateral attempt. Another shallow well had been deepened in 1991 to the Bakken and recovered 1375 barrels of oil before being abandoned. Other wells had attempted horizontal laterals but had failed mechanically. For me, this was good news: it was apparent that oil had been generated and was in the system. But how much oil was there?

For completely different reasons, I was encouraged to discover that a drill stem test had been run on another well in this group that included reservoir pressure measurements. A normally-pressured oil reservoir has a pressure gradient of 0.45 psi/ft (pressure gradient is calculated by dividing the reservoir pressure obtained on a drill-stem test by the depth of the reservoir). In this case, I calculated the reservoir pressure to be 0.52 psi/ft, a slight over-pressuring which could indicate excessive oil generation. So I could chalk up another plus in my new area.

In addition, the log character of the wells in this area appeared similar to the logs of the wells at Elm Coulee field located over 110 miles westward. After the well log study was completed, two key wells stood out from the rest. One, drilled by Gulf Oil in 1982, was the well that showed the slight over-pressuring. The drill-stem test of the Bakken that revealed the over-pressuring also recovered some very small amounts of water-free oil measured in cubic centimeters. The second key well, drilled by Lear Petroleum in 1981, was not cored or tested in the Bakken zone. Several miles south of the Lear well, Mitchell Energy had also drilled a vertical Bakken well in 1981. When I went to Houston to meet with George Mitchell in 2012 (thanks to Chris Pappas), he remembered in great detail the completion attempt that was made on his well. Oil shows were detected in the Middle Bakken. The entire eighty-two foot Bakken interval was perforated and diesel-fracked with poor results. No horizontal drilling attempt was made. It was another opportunity missed.

However, in addition to the logs in this area resembling the logs of Elm Coulee producers, the Bakken zone was also thicker. In addition, the Three Forks reservoir, occurring only fifty feet below the Bakken, had interesting log characteristics with oil shows in a few wells. Balanced against these three pluses were some minuses, which needed further study; but I concluded that this area was promising.

I thought perhaps Walter Arbuckle of Fossil Associates might be interested in this geologic idea since we had connected earlier at Elm Coulee. But he had suffered through a bad experience with lands owned by Indian tribes in southwestern Colorado. When I mentioned that this prospect area included the Fort Berthold Indian Reservation (which covers about 988,000 acres, 46% owned by Native Americans), he was no longer interested.

Discussing Parshall issues with Henry Gordon, 2012.

Then in August 2003, at The Oil and Gas Conference sponsored by Enercom Inc. in Denver, I met Henry Gordon, who was both president of Strata Resources and a stockbroker. He was a good negotiator, very positive and aggressive, and capable of managing acreage acquisitions. He also had connections with oil investors and was seeking someone with solid geologic expertise and creative ideas with whom to partner. A few months later, while still coping with the geological minuses, I showed him my Bakken project. We thought that we would make a good team. We decided to join forces. We would pursue my geologic idea and our relationship would culminate in the most successful venture of our careers.

I still had some misgivings about our first prospect, the acreage surrounding the over-pressured Gulf well. Marathon, a major oil company, had owned a huge leasehold in this area and by the early 1990s, had drilled five Bakken wells, some with free oil recoveries, so they were certainly aware of its potential. I had no explanation for why they allowed these leases to expire.

The importance of geochemical analysis of the Bakken soon became apparent. For example, the poor vitrinite reflectance (Ro) values of the Bakken in this area caused some concern about its maturity (oil-generating capability). Nevertheless some of us believed the high oil content of the Bakken was the cause of the low Ro. It was coating the tiny vitrinite particles present in the shale that come from coal, thus reducing Ro values. Sometime later, however, it became evident that since very little coal is present in the Bakken, little vitrinite would be present, so this issue became less significant.

An even bigger problem was the Rt—or oil saturation of a reservoir based on resistivity. The resistivity of the Middle Bakken reservoir was only 75 to 100 ohms, as determined by the deep curve of the laterolog. At Elm Coulee, our analog, the Bakken reservoir's resistivity was over 1000 ohms, some ten times greater. The high TOC and low Rt did not match. Tmax was also low. The small oil recoveries from Bakken wells in this area could be related to immaturity of the Bakken shales. That brought into play the oil trap that I was proposing, occurring at the juncture of the mature and immature Bakken source beds and forming the eastern boundary of an oil accumulation at a depth of approximately 8750 feet. Such a trap would be unlike any oil trap in the entire Rocky Mountain region. When I sent Dan Jarvie, a good friend and one of the best geochemists in the U.S, a sample of the Bakken shale, he concluded that our area was near the mature-immature boundary. His analysis again raised logical questions about the limited-source issue. This issue continues to confound.

Accurate electric log analysis was complicated by pyrite in the black shales. Pyrite increases bulk density, decreases porosity, and lowers resistivity readings. In addition, although a good measure of organic content, the deep curve of the laterolog is often invaded by drilling mud and does not record true Rt, which may be as much as 30% higher. The shales also contain uranium which affects gamma-ray curve readings. On the positive side, the Bakken shales and the middle member were all thicker than at Elm Coulee, adding value to their potential.

Lineaments (surface topographic features that reflect subsurface structure) were another plus. Lineaments in this part of the Williston Basin are northeast-southwest trending and expressed as drainage anomalies. The Parshall discovery well was drilled on a drainage anomaly formed by Shell Creek, an intermittent stream. Likewise, one of the first wells drilled by Whiting was on a prominent drainage-type lineament feature. The Nesson Anticline is also beautifully expressed topographically (figure 2). These lineaments reflect subsurface faults (with minor displacement, of about five feet) which may have a major horizontal component. They cause fracturing of the reservoirs. The Yellowstone Lineament in Tioga Field is an outstanding example of the beneficial effect of lineaments to oil production (figure 3). Wells located on the lineament have produced over 800,000 barrels, far above the field-well average. One such well's cumulative production exceeds two million barrels. The initial horizontal wells drilled at Parshall were all northwest-trending and designed to intersect these northeast-trending lineament features. Based on seismic data, a few of these faults have a vertical displacement of 30 to 40 feet. Regionally, this area is characterized by a left and right lateral, tilted, wrench-type fault system and also by low-relief structural highs caused by basement faulting with attendant thinning of the overlying stratigraphic section.

The successful horizontal drilling technology at Elm Coulee Field was not common knowledge. There were only a limited number

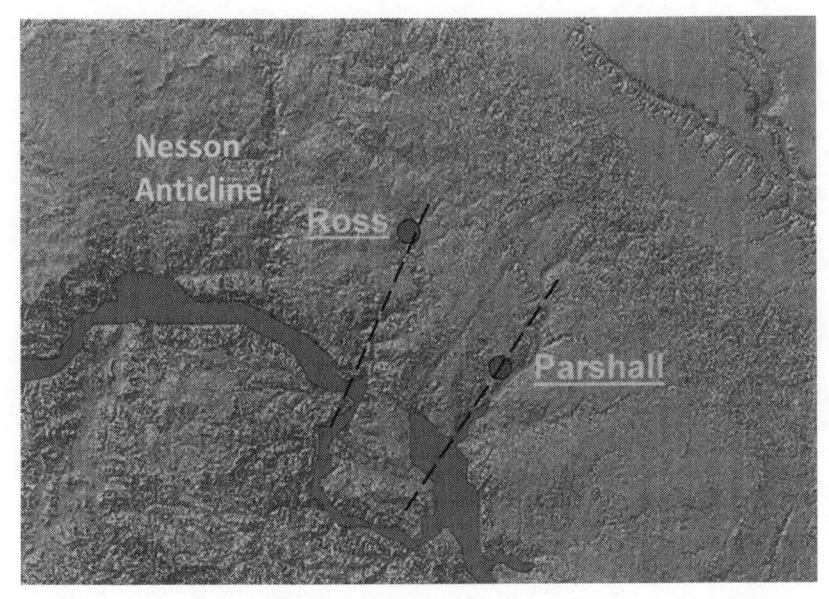

Figure 2. Aerial photograph showing drainage anomalies at Parshall, Ross and the Nesson Anticline. After Anderson, NDGS.

of oil operators with experience in drilling horizontal Bakken wells. However, this new drilling success fit my "new oil-finding technique in a new area" theory. The new technique was horizontal drilling. The new area was the unleased lands in Mountrail County. Taking everything into account, I felt that the potential of the new horizontal-drilling technology, developed some 110 miles westward, outweighed the negative technical data and that we should proceed.

Henry Gordon contracted a leasing crew, and we made our first lease play around the over-pressured Gulf well, one of my two key wells. Starting in May 2004, we leased 5600 acres at a cost of $150,000. Gordon and I each had lease costs of $21,600 and Gordon raised the rest from outside investors. Now that we owned some acreage, we needed to sublease our leases to an oil operator who would be interested in drilling a horizontal Bakken well. Gordon contacted

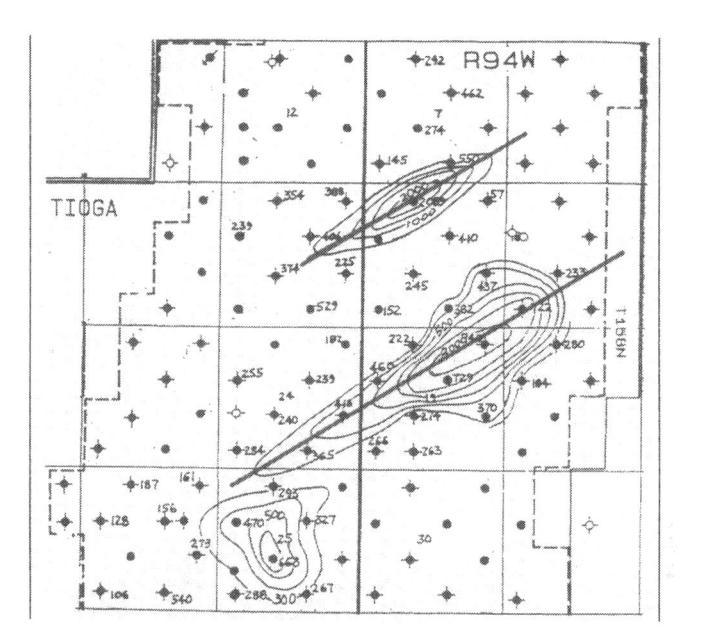

Figure 3. Lineament-enhanced oil production: one 2-million barrel well and another 800,000-barrel well on the Yellowstone Lineament trend. Contour Interval-100,000 bbls.

Jim Powers, President George Solich of Cordillera Energy Partners, and President Don Law of Prima Exploration, Inc. They were following the development of Elm Coulee Field and were interested in getting involved in the Bakken project. They were being advised by Ken Altschuld, whose company was the first to lease lands in the Parshall area. I showed them my geological report, they believed the area had merit and Gordon quickly subleased our acreage to them. They paid us seventy-five dollars per acre plus an overriding royalty interest that included an AMI (area of mutual interest).

During this leasing phase, we ran into a competitor—EOG Resources, Inc., a large Houston-based independent company active in developing Elm Coulee Field. By this time, this company was experienced in drilling horizontal wells in the Bakken Shale and was looking for new areas to explore. Some of their leases were next to ours. EOG was also interested in drilling a Bakken well in this new unexplored area. They contacted Cordillera and Prima about sharing the drilling cost for a horizontally drilled Bakken well. A few months later EOG, Cordillera and Prima formed a drilling unit whereby EOG Resources would serve as the operator and each party agreed to pay a share of the well cost in proportion to its interest in the drilling unit. The well would be named the No.1 Nelson Farms.

In June 2004, Gordon introduced me to a petroleum geologist who was interested in obtaining a substantial interest in a Bakken play. When I met with him, we connected with one another because we had some mutual friends. In a later meeting, the two of us spent several hours together in my office reviewing my Bakken project. We looked at well histories of the twenty-five wells in the area that were already drilled to the Bakken and analyzed the few wells that had reported small oil recoveries. We reviewed Bakken core descriptions and Bakken source rock data. We discussed the Bakken mature-immature problem, the unique oil trap, the low Tmax, the importance of fracture and microfracture porosity, and the effect of salt dissolution. We also analyzed the potential of the underlying Three Forks reservoir, as well as the negatives—the low vitrinite reflectance and the Rt, a measure of oil saturation that was much lower here than at Elm Coulee, our analog. We also focused on the positives: the high TOC values of the Bakken shales (one of the highest in the U.S.), the lineament features, pyrite's effect on log analysis, and the log calculations from Archie's Equation, which showed all wells in this area were oil-productive. He asked questions and I answered them. I felt that the geologic data was impressive. He was already aware of the success of horizontal drilling at Elm Coulee. I then outlined a new area that I thought was prospective, located about twenty miles southward. My area outline covered about 125,000 acres, within which only two or three vertically drilled Bakken wells had been drilled, all in the early 1980s. One of these wells was one of my two key wells in my 2003 geologic study, the Lear Petroleum No. 1 Parshall well. Acreage costs would be minimal because these lands had remained unleased for several years. I suggested that this would be a good place to start. This concluded our several-hour review.

I thought that my story was convincing. We needed financing to buy the acreage covering this prospect and the geologist who would become our partner seemed interested. Gordon and I met with him again and we went over the project in more detail. This was not a project of buying leases and then waiting for the phone to ring; it would be a Bakken geologic play with a well commitment. Not long afterward, our partner agreed to proceed. What he wanted to do was lease a large acreage block. He would pay for all of the leasing costs. He needed help on how to get started and how to implement the project. We would receive a cash commission and an override for my originating the geologic idea and preparing a geologic report, for Gordon's handling the leasing of the acreage, and for our finding a partner and operator to drill a Bakken well.

I placed the eastern boundary of our buy area at a proposed mature-immature boundary of the Bakken Shale. However, that placement was based on problematic and meager data—a 1982 master's thesis by R. L. Webster, then a graduate student at the University of North Dakota, plus one publication from a 1984 guidebook authored by Leigh Price and others, all well-known and very capable geologists. The acreage to be leased would center near the Lear well, the second key well from my 2003 geologic study.

Gordon managed the leasing for the entire project. To handle the onsite leasing, he secured Denver-based Double Deuce Land and Minerals, experienced lease brokers who knew the business well. Lease brokers were in great demand and their daily rate was increasing. We were charged a daily rate that even included Saturdays and Sundays.

Leasing began in fall, 2004. Leases were taken in the name of Gordon's company, Strata Resources. Almost all of the targeted acreage was available. We were the only party leasing in this area. Five-year term leases were purchased for only ten dollars per acre (up to twenty-five dollars later for the holdout mineral owners). The five-year, one-dollar-per-acre rentals were prepaid. For extra compensation, Gordon secured additional three-year options. Nearly all were fee or state lands and fortunately only a few were federally-owned.

By March 2005, still with no competition, approximately 38,200 acres were leased. Strata Resources then assigned the block to our partner, reserving an override. By now, after further study, we were confident that we were pursuing a new, exciting geologic project.

Fortunately, Gordon had also identified additional North Dakota state-owned lands that were unleased in Township 152 and 153 North-Ranges 90 and 91 West. At a state sale held in January 2005, Gordon was the only bidder for 1503 acres. He leased one 80-acre tract for only 93 cents per acre and the rest for one or two dollars per acre! Later, they all produced commercially. Still later, costs for state leases would soar. At a sale held in May 2010, more than $5800 per acre was paid for state leases in this same area. It paid to be there first.

As planned, by March 2005 our partner had secured a large acreage block. His acreage acquisition costs were in the high six-figure range. Well costs would be ten times higher, and he was not interested in bearing the cost of such a risky well venture. Nor did he have the experience to operate the drilling of a horizontal Bakken well. He wanted us to find an experienced oil operator to purchase a 75% interest in the acreage block that we had assembled and to commit to drill a horizontal Bakken well. He wanted to sell this 75% interest at a promoted price to cover his acreage costs and pay for his 25% interest of the initial well cost. We would receive a cash commission if we were able to find an acceptable investor and operator. This offer would terminate on May 20th if no investor was found. Finding such a buyer would be a heavy lift and proved to be a major challenge.

With Elm Coulee field beginning to make the headlines and interest in Bakken prospects increasing, lease speculators were filling the county court offices to check title records. The Bakken play was catching on. Unemployed lease brokers were scarce, and lease prices were soaring. I prepared a 65-slide Power Point presentation that included all of my geological data and engineering and land information, as well as the new horizontal drilling technology being used at Elm Coulee. It was very complete and told a good story. I named it the Parshall Prospect.

As soon as it was completed, in early April 2005, Gordon and I showed my Parshall Prospect presentation incorporating our partner's offering terms to seventeen companies, including some of those active at Elm Coulee. We knew that the primary obstacles we would encounter in marketing this prospect were (1) the few wells that had been drilled, (2) the fact that the nearest commercial Bakken oil production was over 100 miles westward, (3) the large size of the acreage block (which increased the prospect's cost), (4) the Bakken's low-Ro (vitrinite reflectance), which at that time was a major concern, (5) the low 100-ohm resistivity (a measure of oil saturation) of the Bakken reservoir, versus over 1000-ohm resistivity at Elm Coulee, our analog, and (6) the mature-immature boundary problem, including the low Tmax not endemic to source beds like the Bakken. To address this latter problem, I was proposing an oil trap unlike any in the entire Rocky Mountain region.

For companies interested in only a small interest, the first question asked was who would be the operator. We had none. The well and acreage costs were estimated at twelve to fifteen million dollars. For some companies, this amount exceeded their entire Rocky Mountain exploration budget. Some companies meeting with us or attending our presentations were only interested in enriching their knowledge of the Bakken Shale reservoir with my data. Some used my data as a guide and leased lands farther westward. I had luncheon meetings, stopped friends on the street, and exhausted the contacts that I had developed from having a downtown Denver office on the same corner for over fifty-seven years. Gordon had similar results. Our partner's May 20th deadline arrived; he agreed to give us more time but to no avail. In early July 2005, he called. EOG had announced the location of the No. 1 Nelson Farms well that would commence drilling shortly; it was a joint venture with Cordierra and Prima. So our arrangement with our partner ended, perhaps to be renewed after the well was completed.

On July 14, 2005, EOG Resources spud the first horizontal Bakken well to be drilled in this area in twelve years. It was the No.1 Nelson Farms located in Section 24, Township 156 North, 92 West, less than one mile from the Gulf well, one of my two key wells. It was drilled vertically to about 9500 feet; it then angled horizontally to a total depth of 14,433 feet. The well was completed as a poor producer, far below the quality they had hoped for. It was nearly devoid of the siltstone portion of the middle Bakken, one of the main objectives. Strangely, the best recorded oil shows from the mud log were at the contact between the Upper Bakken Shale and the overlying Scallion Limestone at a measured depth interval of 12,200 to 12,400 feet. As of July 2016, this well had produced only 109,430 barrels of oil, with a current daily rate of only fourteen barrels. Of genuinely historic importance, it ranks as one of the most important oil discoveries in North Dakota. It is the discovery well for the horizontally drilled Bakken reservoir in Mountrail County, North Dakota.

The poor results of the Nelson Farms well added very little to the quality of the Parshall Prospect. Our partner called and asked us to try again to get it sold. It was August and five months had lapsed with no success. September and October came and went, still with no success.

Then finally, EOG Resources called our partner in the fall of 2005, asking if the acreage block was still available. EOG wanted to review the prospect with him, so I sent him all the geological data that I had compiled to prepare him for the meeting. A few months later, in early 2006, EOG's landman Ty Stillman and geologist Jim Peterson met with our partner to negotiate the purchase of the Parshall Prospect acreage block. Having mapped the play and the Parshall Prospect area's, Peterson had come to the same conclusion that I had. EOG decided that it was worth pursuing, even at our partner's promoted price and with his challenging terms (namely, a commitment to drilling a horizontal well). To this day I don't know the price paid by EOG Resources for the acreage block. It took ten months of grueling effort by Gordon and me to reach this stage of development for the Parshall Prospect. Our efforts were finally rewarded. We received a cash commission. We had worked closely together throughout the prospect phase. Gordon and I simply had a 50%-50% handshake deal with only a few, short, hand-written agreements.

The assignment of the acreage block from our partner to EOG Resources is dated February 9, 2006, with a recorded date of March 17th. Our task was over, and we eagerly anticipated the drilling of the well.

Our prospect now belonged to EOG Resources, an offshoot of Enron. Because of Enron's financial implosion in December 2001, EOG was unusually tight-lipped about releasing information. We were not going to receive any information on their well. In addition, because our agreement did not include an area of mutual interest (AMI), any leases purchased by either party after the date of the contract were not shared but belonged to the lessor.

The two key wells from my 2003 geological study would become the locale of the first two wells to be drilled in the Bakken play. EOG started their evaluation of the Parshall acreage block by conducting a 3-D seismic program surrounding their proposed drill site. Later they staked the No. 1-36 Parshall well in Section 36 Township 153 North Range 90 West, only several hundred feet from the Lear well drilled in 1981. Their well spud on April 11, 2006. It was planned as a 14,500-foot, northwest-trending, horizontal-lateral well. However, at a measured depth (horizontal and vertical distance) of 9718 feet, the well encountered extremely high reservoir pressure. That certainly must have caused some excitement for EOG Resources. This occurred on April 27, 2006. The well reached a total depth of only 11,325 feet. Extremely high reservoir pressure precluded further drilling. It was completed in May 2006, from a 1600-foot lateral, producing 463 barrels of oil per day. As the discovery well for Parshall Field, it deserves to be long remembered because of its significance to the oil industry in the Rocky Mountain region.

A second well, drilled in the same Section 36 less than one mile from the discovery well, encountered a similar high reservoir pressure problem and was also completed from a short horizontal lateral of approximately 2500 feet. The third well—the EOG Resources No.1-03H Bartelson, located one mile southward—is the first successful completion from a long horizontal lateral, at a total measured depth of 14,900 feet. The main pay zone for Parshall Field became the dolomite in the lower part of the middle member of the Bakken (not the overlying siltstone), the top of which occurs at a depth of 9610 feet and is easily identified by a characteristic gamma ray marker. It was completed for 628 barrels of oil per day. As of July 2016 this well had produced 503,160 barrels.

It is of historic interest that, according to North Dakota Oil and Gas Division records, on April 24, 2006 (i.e., prior to the Parshall discovery), Whiting Petroleum Corporation completed their Sanish Area Bakken discovery, the No.1 Bartleson, located in Section 1-Township 152 North-Range 93 West, about sixteen miles westward.

This completes my Parshall discovery story as mentioned in the preface. What followed is well documented by the thousands of articles written in magazines, periodicals, books, and newspapers and by talks given at meetings, conferences, symposiums, and lectures.

EOG Resources needs to be commended for undertaking these huge financial risks. They first participated, at considerable cost, in drilling the marginally-commercial Nelson Farms well. This was followed by purchasing, at a promoted price, the 38,200-acre block belonging to our partner. It then took three costly wells to finally confirm the Parshall oil field discovery. Their reward was discovery of a major oil field, one of the largest in North America.

Drilling and leasing activity took off at a frenzied pace. Because many of the leases in Parshall Prospect would expire in less than four years, drilling surged. Our partner had a financial problem. He had participated in paying for his 25% interest in the first three EOG wells. Hundreds of drilling obligations were looming, creating an overwhelming financial burden for him. He was interested in finding a capable buyer but also one that would be a good partner for EOG Resources. He sold his interest to Whiting Petroleum Corporation.

Wells were being completed at rates of over 1000 barrels per day. Geologist Ed Dolly passed me on the street one day and told me of one Bakken completion that was completed at a rate of 200 barrels per hour! What was also true was that these high initial production rates declined rapidly. After a few months, the production rate would be much less than half of the initial rate. Because of the high oil price, however, payout of these wells occurred in less than a year, with some paying out in less than six months. Lands were being leased for thousands of dollars per acre. When Bartleson, the royalty owner of the original Bartleson well, was asked months later what was the first thing he was going to do with his first royalty check totaling several hundred thousand dollars, he replied, "I'm going to fix the door on my pickup truck."

A multi-rig program began, and soon horizontal Bakken producers filled the original projected limits of the field. However, the field continued to grow in size. More drilling rigs were added; more companies became involved. Surprisingly, by 2008, the field covered more than 360,000 acres, and discovered oil reserves were calculated at 250 million barrels.

By June 2009, the field size had increased even further: it covered 1,100,000 acres, with 1900 completed wells and reserves estimated at 700 million barrels. On the New York Stock Exchange, EOG Resources stock doubled, then split and rose again; three other major Bakken oil operators—Whiting Petroleum Corporation, Continental Resources, and Kodiak Oil and Gas—also enjoyed excellent runs.

Yet another new reservoir, the Three Forks dolomite (long suspected as being commercial), was discovered only fifty feet deeper than the Bakken, with three separate pay zones. It added huge additional reserves but in a more limited area than the Bakken. North Dakota's single most prolific horizontal-oil producer is an unfracked Three Forks well, the USA No. 2D-3-1H, operated by Petro-Hunt USA on the east flank of Charlson Field in Section 2-Township 153 North-Range 95 West. It has produced over 1.52 million barrels and is still producing 175 bopd. More important, it soon became evident that because of the nature of these two reservoirs, one well for every spacing unit of 640 acres would be insufficient to drain the huge amount of oil in the rock. In these richer zones, more wells per spacing unit (which would be enlarged to 1280 acres) would be needed. Thousands of new development wells would be required. By August 2012, Parshall's size, number of wells, and reserves were astronomical.

It became evident that Parshall fit the concept of a huge unconventional resource play—that is, 1) a huge and continuous oil accumulation that covers millions of acres, 2) no clearly defined oil-water contacts, 3) overpressure, 4) sweet spots of production, 5) low water

Parshall Field, Badlands topography, northeast of Killdeer, North Dakota. Little Missouri River in background; Lake Sakakawea at top of photo.

production, and 6) rich source rocks and poor quality reservoir rocks. It is a closed system 160 feet thick and extends from the top of the Upper Bakken shale to 70 feet into the Three Forks formation. The reservoirs average less than 7% porosity and less than one millidarcy permeability. The Tmax is 440°C west of Parshall and lowers to 420°C at Parshall, where it is still considered to be immature. Short distance migration is indicated. Hydrogen Index (a measure of the type or hydrocarbon-generating capacity of organic matter in a rock) is about 150 west of Parshall and over 650 east of Parshall at the barrier.

When the North Dakota Oil and Gas Division released its parameters for the field in 2012, it showed that Parshall had grown in size to six million acres (9400 square miles), requiring 37,000 wells to fully develop the Bakken and Three Forks reservoirs. One hundred seventy-five active rigs were developing the field; 7600 wells had been completed and were producing 725,000 barrels of oil per

Fully developed portion of Parshall Field (20 pads), Great Plains topography.

Parshall Field, showing glacial topography. Laterals are drilled under Lake Sakakawea (courtesy of Whiting Oil and Gas Corp., ©2010 Jim Blecha Photography, Inc.).

Hess loop-track oil tank car facility looking northeast,
Tioga in the background.

Four Bear Village and Four Bear Bridge,
the only nearby crossing of Lake Sakakawea.

day. By early 2014, some 8400 wells had been completed and daily production had increased to 1.025 million barrels per day and was increasing monthly. By September 2015, even after the dramatic drop in crude oil price, an additional 1300 wells had been completed (including 925 wells waiting on completion services) and daily oil production was close to an all-time high of 1.2 million barrels.

By 2016, new estimates by the North Dakota Oil and Gas Division of total wells necessary to fully develop Parshall Field increased to 55,000 to 65,000 wells, which would increase previous recoverable oil reserve estimates by a large margin. My estimate of recoverable oil reserves for Parshall Field is in excess of fifteen billion barrels not including gas equivalents. The U.S. leads the world in oil and gas technology and in technological breakthroughs in other industries as well. That is why these reserve figures will be met and will increase in the future with new completion practices and fracking techniques, and by secondary recovery methods. My reserve figure is less than five percent of the 413 billion barrels of oil in place as determined in an unpublished report by expert geochemist Leigh Price. It should also be noted that the Bakken is a closed system and generated oil has not migrated out into other reservoirs.

The second largest oil-producing state, North Dakota has surpassed California and Alaska, and Parshall would resemble Prudhoe Bay, Eagle Ford and the Spraberry-Wolfcamp fields as one of the largest North American oil fields. Internationally, comparing Parshall to the other giant oil fields of the world, it is one of the top twenty, based on my research.

Parshall Field operators have compensated mineral owners (individual landowners, the state and Native Americans) with large incomes from lease bonuses and royalties. Among the mineral owners, the federal government sometimes burdens its mineral interests

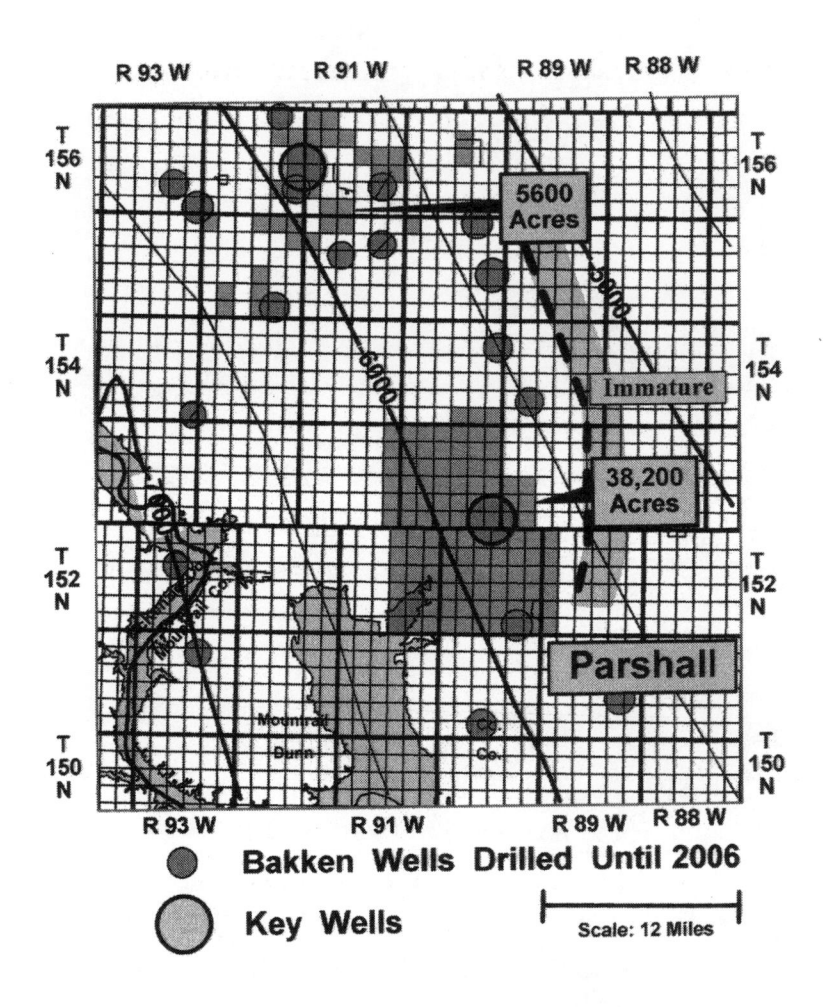

Plate V. Bakken Wells Drilled Until 2006.

with onerous stipulations that reduce development; fortunately federal lands are minimal. Though increased economic prosperity has brought on water shortages, housing issues and increased crime and other social problems, the positives far outweigh the negatives. North Dakota's unemployment has been reduced, the state has

PARSHALL FIELD: A CAREER TURNING-POINT

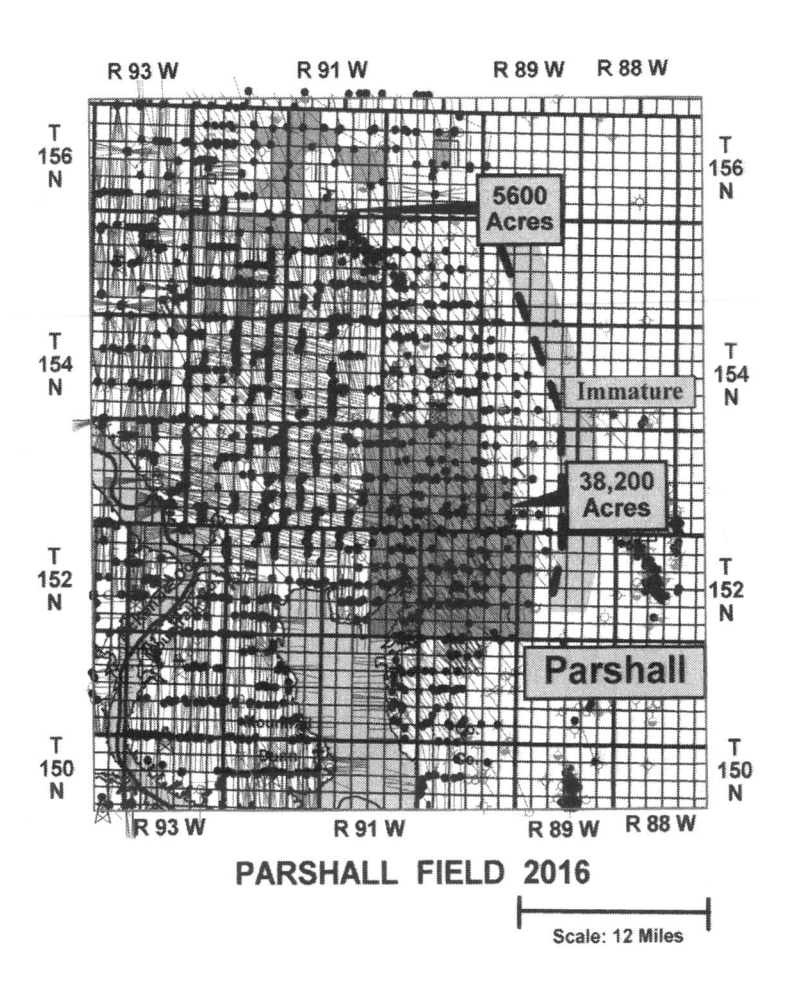

Plate VI. Parshall Field 2016. Diagonal, horizontal and vertical lines indicate wells. Dots indicate surface locations.

a GDP far above the national average, and it enjoys a billion-dollar state budget surplus.

And all of this started with my 2003 geologic study, pinpointing two key wells destined to become the discovery wells for this super giant oil field. Plate V shows the area in 2006; plate VI shows the area in 2016.

The field's size has astounded the oil industry (plate VII). Its unique feature is the trap (what caused the oil to accumulate) at the mature-immature boundary of the Bakken shales; it is also a stratigraphic trap, as proposed by the fine geologic staff at Whiting, headed by Vice President Mark Williams. I am not aware of any other oil trap of this type in the Rocky Mountain region. Comparable horizontal drilling technology has become a model for fifteen to twenty new projects elsewhere in the U.S. What started as a one-man band has grown to a large symphony orchestra. Significantly, in the near future, reliance on imported oil will decrease. Domestic oil reserves could almost double in the coming years.

PARSHALL FIELD: A CAREER TURNING-POINT

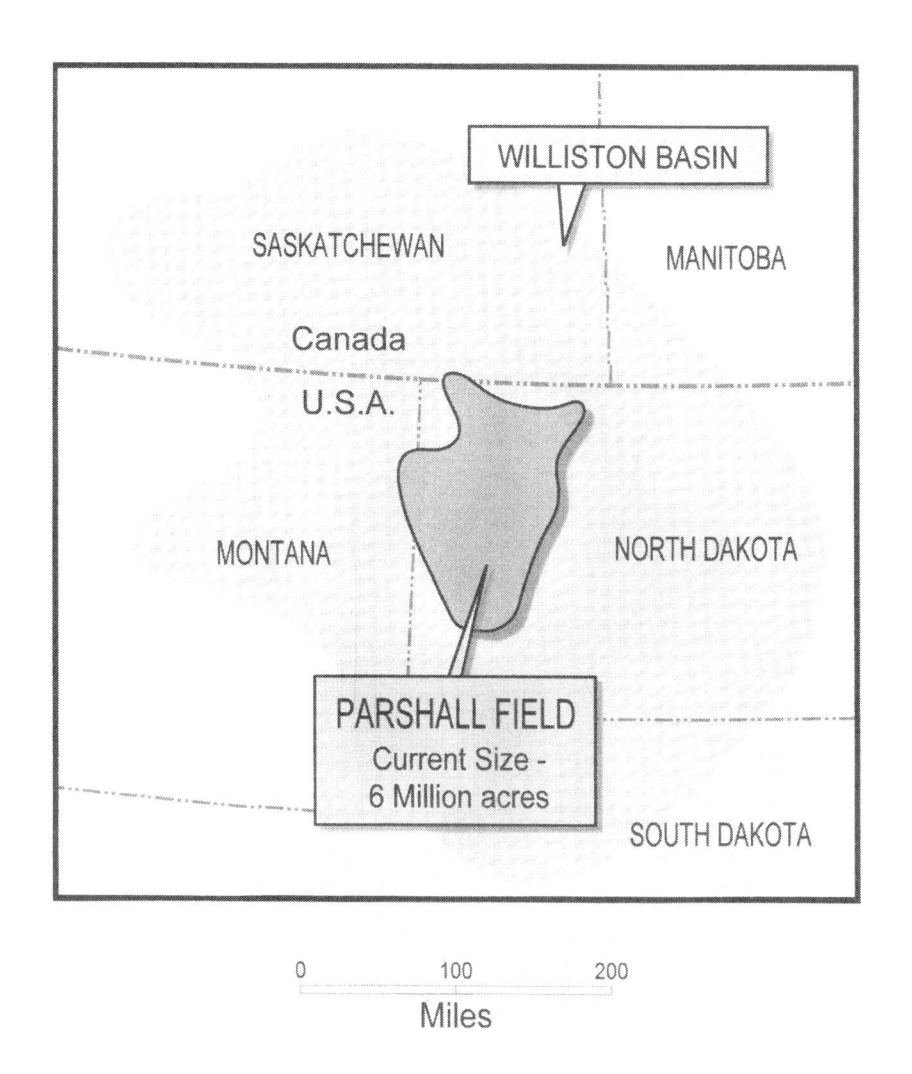

Plate VII. PARSHALL FIELD--CURRENT SIZE: 6 million acres.

THE GEOLOGIC IDEA

Soon after Parshall began to expand, in the fall of 2006, several oil companies that had missed out on Parshall called and were asking if I had any other Bakken ideas. Where was the next Parshall?

The hunt was on. All of the sedimentary basins in the U.S. were undergoing critical review. Equipped with horizontal drilling technology, a revolution in domestic oil and gas exploration was beginning.

In August 2006, I was thumbing through the *Geologic Atlas of the Rocky Mountain Region,* a classic volume published by RMAG in 1972, nicknamed The Big Red Book. It is 21 by 18 inches in size and contains hundreds of figures, maps and cross-sections relating to the geology of the entire Rocky Mountain region. Its 331 pages of text took years of preparation. On page 98 was a map showing areas where Bakken-type rocks were present in the Rockies. In addition to the Parshall area covering western North Dakota, eastern

Montana, and parts of Alberta and Saskatchewan, there was, surprisingly, another area. It had gone unnoticed. For me, it was a new Bakken area, a new idea. It was located about 490 miles west of Parshall in eastern Glacier County, Montana.

The geologic setting was similar to Parshall. After reviewing several wells drilled to the Bakken zone from the 1970s to early 1990s, I realized that the well logs and other well data of Parshall and this new area were almost identical. Horizontal drilling had never been attempted. Based on the analysis of the rock cuttings that I sent to Dan Jarvie for evaluation, the TOC of the Bakken shales calculated high enough to be commercially viable. Henry Gordon, again my partner, made a preliminary land check and found that there had not been any recent leasing activity and virtually none of the prospective acreage was leased. Everything looked positive.

It was a good geologic idea; I named it Whitegrass Prospect. Such ideas can be very valuable and rewarding. Such was the case at Parshall. They are closely guarded and require quick action before they are discovered by other companies. This type of thinking applies not only to the oil industry but to all industries. What Gordon and I needed was a large independent company with a capable staff whom we could trust to undertake leasing a large acreage block, perhaps 100,000 acres or more, and reward us for the geologic idea with a cash commission and an overriding royalty interest in all acreage leased. It would be a big task to secure such a company.

We first thought of showing Whitegrass to Robert Armstrong, a petroleum engineer who was acquisitions manager in Denver for a large independent oil company headquartered in Louisiana. I had known Armstrong for many years when he was employed by Westport Energy and I had an interest in a horizontally drilled

THE GEOLOGIC IDEA

Madison well at Elkhorn Ranch Field drilled by Conoco in 1991 and later acquired by Westport in January 1995. I called him occasionally to get updates on the well's production. He was interested in any Bakken project that I developed. We felt that we could trust him with the idea. His would be the first company to see Whitegrass.

Gordon and I presented Whitegrass to Armstrong in September 2006. The geologic similarity to Parshall was appealing. His company was in a buying mood and liked the idea. It took fewer than ten days for them to commit to Whitegrass. What a stroke of luck! Past success is sometimes rewarded. An area of interest was formed covering over 300,000 acres. Agreements were quickly signed and leasing began. Early in the leasing phase, it turned out that a large portion of our buying area was tribal lands belonging to the Blackfeet Indian tribe. Their leases required a larger royalty than the 12.5% ordinarily paid to lessees. Gordon renegotiated our trade. We agreed to reduce our override in order to accommodate the tribal royalty requirement. We ended up receiving a cash commission of $100,000 plus ten dollars per acre for the first 40,000 acres leased and an override on all acreage leased. We were very satisfied with the terms. Gordon had made a good trade. My half of the $500,000 commission was the largest I had ever received in my entire career. It demonstrated the value of a good geologic idea, one generated by reviewing a forty-year-old publication.

They proceeded to lease a total of 138,000 gross acres. Horizontal Bakken wells were drilled that revealed the reservoir was of much poorer quality than originally conceived. Rosetta Exploration, Inc. and Newfield Exploration Company followed our entry and later leased lands in other parts of our prospective area; their horizontal wells confirmed the poor quality of the Bakken reservoir. An unusual source bed problem, not fully addressed initially, might have partly contributed to the project failure. Some new completion techniques were tried and some wells were completed as oil producers but they quickly depleted. The project was a disappointment and was soon abandoned.

Much more important, however, our Bakken idea was pursued with huge success some thirty-five miles northeastward into Alberta, Canada by independent Canadian oil companies. In the past few years, in a separate geologic setting, companies such as Dee Three Exploration Ltd and Granite Oil Corporation have discovered and developed some 100,000 acres of Bakken production at the Ferguson Field area, extending over thirty miles, with in-place oil figures of hundreds of millions of barrels. My geologic idea was valid. Unfortunately, it was not productive where it was originally conceived.

CAREER ACHIEVEMENTS REWARDED

With success has come recognition and honors. Since November 2007, I have given over twenty talks on Parshall Field throughout the United States. I have been stunned at the public's lack of knowledge about Parshall and its significance.

In September 2008, I learned I was to receive the ultimate award in my profession. Scott Tinker, AAPG president, called to congratulate me for being selected to receive the AAPG 2009 Outstanding Explorer Award. It is an honor bestowed by the world's largest geological association, comprised of more than 38,000 members from more than 135 countries. With all of my family attending, I was presented with the award in a Denver ceremony on June 9, 2009. Previously, in late 2008, I received the prestigious Outstanding Explorer Award offered annually by the RMAG, the largest geological society in the Rocky Mountain region, with three thousand members. In 2014, the RMAG honored me further by renaming

Kay, Hunter, J. Michael and Mike, 2012.

RMAG Explorer of the Year Award, 2008.

CAREER ACHIEVEMENTS REWARDED

AAPG Explorer of the Year Award, Denver, June, 2009.

With Scott Tinker, AAPG President, Denver, June, 2009.

their explorer award The Michael S. Johnson Outstanding Explorer Award. Also in late 2014, joining a group that included presidents of Continental Resources and Whiting Petroleum Corporation, I was selected as one of twenty 2014 honorees and inducted into the Western Energy Alliance Rocky Mountain Hall of Fame, an honor recognizing Rocky Mountain oil leaders.

One outstanding Hall of Fame member who has excelled in more than one Rocky Mountain oil endeavor and who is respected by all is Bill Barrett, a longtime friend from my Casper days. His major success was in Colorado's Piceance Basin in the unconventional Williams Fork, tight-sandstone, gas reservoir where his company completed several hundred gas wells, developing over two tcf (trillion cubic feet) of gas reserves plus several tcf of probable/possible gas reserves. He was also involved in the coalbed methane play in the Powder River Basin that yielded 25 tcf of gas reserves and the Madden Field in the Wind River Basin with multi-trillion gas reserves. His company also had interests in the 60-million-barrel Red Wing Creek oil field in North Dakota where the trap was formed by an impact crater (astrobleme).

His company, Barrett Energy Corp., was formed in 1981 with stock trading for 38 cents per share. Barrett went public in 1984, was listed on the NYSE in 1994 and sold to the Williams Companies for 2.8 billion dollars in 2001 at over 73 dollars per share. His is an enviable record.

Over the span of my domestic career, notwithstanding disruptions for military service and foreign intrigues, I have had the good fortune of earning an interest in oil and gas production from a number of oil fields, nearly all located in the Rockies.

This began in 1973 in the Souris Southwest oil field located in Bottineau County, north central North Dakota, while I was working with Tiddens Petroleum Company. Some 42 years later, these wells still bring a few dollars monthly. Also in North Dakota, using my many years of Amerada experience in studying the Nesson Anticline oil fields, I developed oil income there from several oil fields. Three of them were at Capa, Lost Bridge, and Oakdale. The fourth was an extension to Tioga Field, North Dakota's second oil field, discovered in 1951. The discovery well, the No. 1 Henry O. Bakken, is where the Bakken name originated. It is also the discovery well for the Madison reservoir, one of North Dakota's largest. Then, together with Jim Snider (formerly chief geologist of Amerada, who later excelled with Hamilton Brothers Oil Company), we discovered the fifth field at Rattlesnake Point, a million-barrel, one-well oil field. Some twenty years later, with the newly-discovered Bakken production, reserves exceed three million barrels. The sixth and last field of this group was at Bear Creek: Mesa Petroleum beat us to the discovery but Wessely-Headington was able to participate in three oil producers. Later when my purse was seriously depleting, I sold my overriding royalty interest in Bear Creek for the equivalent of

With Rocky Mountain legend Bill Barrett.

a five-year payout, which ranks as the worst decision of my career. With an assist from a successful water flood and additional Bakken development, Bear Creek is still producing at a high rate twenty-eight years later.

In Montana, the tiny mineral interests acquired at Elm Coulee Field all produced, but more important, led to the study of Parshall Prospect and discovery of Parshall Field, my ultimate triumph. Over 441 Bakken oil producers have been completed on the acreage block that was subleased to EOG Resources in 2006.

Wyoming's South Bishop Ranch field, which I discovered with Wessely-Headington, was a home run that helped launch my consulting career. My 2% override paid many bills for eight years, after which in 1976, I sold this interest to Tip Polumbus for $160,000.

One of the few successes during my Apache years was a Colorado J sand discovery in the Denver Julesburg Basin. Named Pat Field, it was a bright spot in an otherwise uneventful Apache tenure.

In New Mexico, the two federal leases that Kay won in the federal lottery in the 1960s were a surprise bonus: they are still producing fifty years later.

Along with success has come fortune. Kay and I have been blessed with good fortune and believe that we should give back to the community and gladly do so. We hope that our giving has eased the lives of some of those in our community who are less privileged than we are. Life is fuller when you do things for others. We feel that charitable giving is Christian faith in action. We like to make poor and needy people happy. We support our church in numerous ways: through membership in Leadership 100 and FAITH (a charity funded at the highest levels), and recently by funding a $2-million-dollar chapel addition. Also, for more than ten years,

CAREER ACHIEVEMENTS REWARDED

Kay, Mike, Alicia and Michael at black-tie affair,
Denver Museum of Nature and Science, 2012.

Kay volunteered her services to CASA (Court Appointed Special Advocates), her favorite charity; as a couple, we are one of its major supporters. Our giving also supports Denver scholarship funds, the Denver Museum of Nature and Science, and other charities. The Denver Foundation will receive the largest portion of our estate, to further some twenty charitable causes.

Not only has my career been interesting, fulfilling and financially rewarding. I have also enjoyed the challenging search for significant oil and gas reserves. This quest has required mastering geologic data, developing innovative ideas, pursuing the most promising prospects, preparing and presenting compelling proposals to the industry, securing support for prospects—and then experiencing both the thrill of oil discoveries and the disappointment of dry holes. My fascination with petroleum geology has made it possible for me to enjoy competing in this roller-coaster oil industry. The industry's inherently high risk requires perseverance and tenacity; honesty and intelligence make it possible to compete with integrity and skill. My journey has convinced me that regardless of your original circumstances, it is self-defeating to believe that you cannot succeed. An old adage in the oil business rightly claims that "those who take the biggest risk get the biggest reward". That was certainly true for EOG Resources, when it took on the risky Parshall Prospect at a cost of more than twelve million dollars. Actual cost might be three times this figure since it took three wells to completely verify this discovery. Their reward was the discovery of a major oil field.

Stompin' in tall cotton at Rocky Mountain Hall of Fame, 2014, with (from left): Peterson, President, Kodiak; Hamm, President, Continental Resources; Isaacs, President, RIM Operating Companies; Mike; Petrie, President, Petrie Partners.

CAREER ACHIEVEMENTS REWARDED

Mike (2nd from left) and Dean Spanos (far right), representing family owners of the Chargers and hosting FAITH meeting in San Diego.

A framed admonition has always hung on my office wall and on my son's as well. It faithfully reflects my business outlook:

THE PRICE OF SUCCESS

I often wonder what it is that brings one man success in life, and what it is that brings mediocrity or failure to his brother. The difference can't be in mental capacity; there is not the difference in our mentalities indicated by the difference in performance. In short, I have reached the conclusion that some men succeed because they cheerfully pay the price of success, and others, tho they may claim ambition and a desire to succeed, are unwilling to pay that price.

AND THE PRICE IS

To use all your courage to force yourself to concentrate on the problem in hand, to think of it deeply and constantly, to study it from all angles, and to plan: To have high and sustained determination to put over what you plan to accomplish, not if circumstances be favorable to its accomplishment, but in spite of all adverse circumstances which may arise—and nothing worthwhile has even been accomplished without some obstacles having been overcome.

To refuse to believe that there are any circumstances sufficiently strong to defeat you in the accomplishment of your purpose. Hard? I should say so. That's why so many men never attempt to acquire success, answer the siren call of the rut and remain on the beaten paths that are for beaten men. Nothing worthwhile has ever been achieved without constant endeavor, some pain and constant application of the lash of ambition.

That's the price of success as I see it. And I believe every man should ask himself: Am I willing to endure the pain of this struggle for the comforts and the rewards and the glory that go with achievement? Or shall I accept the uneasy and inadequate contentment that comes with mediocrity? Am I willing to pay the Price of Success?

And the Time to Begin to Pay is Now

—Copyright, Alexander Hamilton Institute, 1926

Sixteen years before this poem's publication, in April 1910, President Teddy Roosevelt gave a similarly-themed speech at the Sorbonne in Paris:

It is not the critic who counts; not the man who points out how the strong man stumbles, or where the doer of deeds could have done them better. The credit belongs to the man who is actually in the arena, whose face is marred by dust and sweat and blood; who strives valiantly; who errs, and comes short again and again, because there is no effort without error or shortcoming; but who does actually strive to do the deeds; who knows the great enthusiasms, the great devotions; who spends himself in a worthy cause; who at the best knows in the end the triumph of high achievement, and who at the worst, if he fails, at least fails while daring greatly, so that his place shall never be with those cold and timid souls who know neither victory nor defeat.

Sometimes at meetings or over dinner, I have asked my companions why America is the world's leader and the most admired country in the world. Continents such as South America and Africa, and countries like China and Russia, share a climate, fertile farm lands, and mineral wealth similar to the United States'; the difference is that we have a unique government. Its founding, philosophical pillars allow individuals to fulfill their quest for business freedom and independence. Our Constitution allows us entrepreneurship—the right to try things for ourselves, to take risks, to benefit from our successes, and to enjoy the satisfaction of achievement. If adversity comes our way, we can take the opportunity and muster the courage to try again, overcoming any government regulations or other obstacles.

Our type of government owes a great deal to a long-ago predecessor. In 500 B.C. the Athenians gave birth to Western philosophy and a democracy that fostered free speech, trial by jury, civilian control over the military, deliberation and forethought, and other principles. They valued their freedoms as much as they valued their families, and this freedom did not come free. For most of that century, Athenians were at war for two out of every three years.

A similar situation confronts us and the world today. I firmly believe that each of us should try to contribute to the betterment of society. With some geological expertise and a lot of luck, I have been able to contribute to our country's domestic oil supply. We should also try to leave our children and grandchildren a better world so that they can live in peace and prosperity. Unfortunately our government has deteriorated to the point that fewer than 30% of its people believe in its competence to legislate wisely. Part of this declining confidence can be traced to our nineteen-trillion-dollar debt (and growing): if you string together one trillion dollars' worth of one-hundred dollar bills, they will circle the earth thirty-eight times.[xxv] Fiscal responsibility is a must for our future.

My professional career and financial success were not a birthright. I grew up living frugally and still remember the tough times when money was scarce. I remember my fifteen-dollar suit and walking for blocks to Tulsa's Wonder Bakery to save our family a nickel by buying day-old bread. My father died when I was a teenager. My mother, unschooled, taught me morality and gave me her devoted attention. However, with little outside guidance, it was up to me in my formative years to find my way and compete with many others more privileged than I was. Perseverance and tenacity have been my watch words. My instinct is to seek solutions, rather than spend time complaining about problems. In my later years, I still enjoy challenges and investing my time in worthwhile projects, preferring the fulfillment they provide, compared to just relaxing, sipping wine in an easy chair. I finish reading a book every few months. Our country is flooded with new arrivals on top of many existing classics on every subject imaginable. A fascinating book that I have read three times is Bill Bryson's *A Short History of Nearly Everything*. I also enjoy reading classical history, spy thrillers, nonfiction about WWII and, of course, success stories.

Part of the purpose of this memoir is to help readers achieve success in their endeavors through my example. Four turning-points in my professional life made all the difference, starting with Rodger Denison giving me my first job at Amerada. Later, I resisted the temptation of a glamorous life in Washington, D.C. and returned to work as a petroleum geologist in Williston, North Dakota. Then when I was thirty-two, Ted Bartling hired me to run Apache's operations in the Rockies. After that, the Wessely-Headington years built my confidence as an oil-finder when South Bishop Ranch field was discovered.

Much later in life, I enjoyed the ultimate in financial success, thanks to my highest professional achievement—participating in the discovery of the Parshall oil field. Equally important to me is the peer recognition I have received and the knowledge that my accomplishments have benefited our country. I have few regrets.

My father came to America as a poor Greek immigrant. He and my mother not only raised me to aspire to great heights, but also gave me the opportunity to succeed. I was able in one generation to go from Obscurity to Success in the Oil Business. I have lived the American Dream.

Only in America.

POSTSCRIPT

Revisiting past moments and experiences in our lives and capturing them in writing are difficult challenges. My thanks go to Kay for enduring the isolation that I imposed on her so I could recall and recount my life's events. She also edited and contributed to the stories of some of our shared experiences. My daughter Alicia and her husband Michael worked computer magic to compile the text in proper form, offering many helpful comments along the way, and I thank them for that.

The idea of writing an autobiography came from John Peterson, who had just finished his, and I thank him for that and our fifty-eight years of friendship. Kathlene Sutton is a master at reading, correcting, reviewing and adding to texts. She took some of my prose and turned it into Shakespeare.

It is amazing how much encyclopedic knowledge I accessed with my iPhone. While browsing Google, I found three pages about the small Greek village that my parents came from. My iPhone held a wealth of information on the 1921 Tulsa race riot, which was unknown to me despite spending fifteen years of my life there. Google supplied details of the atomic tests at the Nevada Test Site, and the Utah Geological Survey provided some of the data on the oil shales and shale oils. Walter Johnson drafted the section on seismic data in the Notes and it is excellent. The Headington Oil Company in Dallas furnished the photograph of our arrival in Yape, Panama, and I thank John Robinson for pointing out some critical errors in the original text on oil deposits and energy policy. I received critical help from Don Todd, who critiqued my account of his Indonesian experience, and also from Joe Brinkman, who supplied me with detailed data on the North Sea venture. Robert Weimer, Paul Weimer, Bill Barrett, Stephen Sonnenberg and Lynn Helms read the book and their comments enriched its content. Numerous Parshall statistics come from the North Dakota Oil and Gas Division, the finest such organization in the Rockies, capably headed by Lynn Helms. My energy figures are compatible with data from Jeffries, J. P. Morgan, ExxonMobil, EIA, and Google.

The few remaining photos of my parents and my childhood are treasured: I am fortunate that they have withstood the rigors of time. My awards, plaques, and mementos remain in my office, a constant reminder of my good fortune. For all of this, I am eternally grateful.

NOTES

i. In 1897, while Oklahoma was still part of the Indian Territory, oil was discovered near Tulsa. By 1905 the huge Red Fork and Glenn Pool discoveries were made nearby, and Tulsa became an oil boomtown. In 1907 Oklahoma became the nation's 46th state, and Tulsa was known as the "Oil Capital of the World." During World War I, petroleum's value attained new heights, and Tulsa gained new importance. It became headquarters to hundreds of oil-related companies. Stanolind (now BP), Amerada Petroleum Corporation, my first employer (later merged with Hess), Carter Oil Company (now ExxonMobil), Cities Service Oil (now Citgo), Sinclair and others all had offices in Tulsa.

Smaller companies like Warren Petroleum Corporation, Reading and Bates, Helmerich and Payne, Skelly Oil Company and others, along with independent geologists and landmen, joined in the oil boom. Oil brought prosperity and philanthropy. Waite Phillips, a successful Tulsa oil pioneer, would donate his huge estate to the city; it became the Philbrook Museum. Other notable residents included Harry Sinclair, Bill Skelly and J. Paul Getty. Tulsa's southeast side would become one of the classiest neighborhoods in the U.S. In the nearby cities of Bartlesville and Enid, Conoco-Phillips had its beginnings. E.W. Marland, oil pioneer and owner of Marland Oil Company in Enid, acquired the Continental Oil and Transportation Company; the company changed its name to Continental Oil Company, later shortened to Conoco. Meanwhile, in the early 1900s, brothers Frank and L. E. Phillips started Phillips Oil Company (later named Phillips 66) in nearby Bartlesville. Phillips was the first company to extract liquid products, such as distillates, from natural gas; up until then, natural gas was flared and wasted in the production of oil. Much of Phillips 66's later success can be traced to its early patents and huge profits based on this innovation. In 2002 Phillips merged with Conoco, to become Conoco-Phillips, the world's fifth-largest private-sector energy corporation. Now headquartered in Houston, its capital assets top 150 billion dollars.

ii. My RMAG publication, appearing in *The Mountain Geologist* and entitled "Discovery of Oil in the Williston Basin: Story of the #1 Clarence Iverson Well" (Vol. 38, No.4, October 2001, pp. 165-180), explains in detail the Iverson oil discovery.

iii. The drill-stem test is a procedure for determining the potential productivity of an oil and gas reservoir by measuring fluid recoveries and reservoir pressures. A tool is attached to the drill pipe that measures reservoir pressures and includes packers to isolate the zone to be tested, plus a chamber to collect a fluid sample. If the formation pressure is sufficient, oil, gas, or water flows into and fills the drill pipe. When the drill pipe is pulled out of the hole, the gas, fluid type, and amounts are recorded.

iv. Athelstan Spilhaus (1911-1998) was the technical director of the testing program. After graduating from the University of Cape Town in 1931, he settled permanently in the U.S. He earned a master's degree from MIT and later returned to Cape Town for his doctorate. A geophysicist and meteorologist, he joined the Woods Hole Oceanographic Institution in Massachusetts, where he developed the bathythermograph. This device made it possible to measure ocean depths and also temperature differences caused by a moving vessel; it proved indispensable to submarine warfare in WWII. He later became dean of the University of Minnesota's Institute of Technology. An inventor and author of hundreds of technical articles, he deservedly considered himself a genius. When asked how to win at Las Vegas' craps tables, he concluded, after a detailed study, that the only way to win was to be "the house," the club owner.

v. Operation Buster-Jangle

Date	Size	Type of Delivery	Title
10/22/51	0.1 KT	From 100-ft. Tower	Able
10/28/51	3.5 KT	Airdrop	Baker
10/30/51	14.0 KT	Airdrop	Charlie
11/1/51	21.0 KT	Airdrop	Dog
11/5/51	31.0 KT	Airdrop	Easy
11/19/51	1.2 KT	Airdrop	Sugar
11/29/51	1.2 KT	Crater	Uncle

Operation Tumbler-Snapper

Date	Size	Type of Delivery	Title
4/1/52	1 KT	Airdrop	Able
4/15/52	1 KT	Airdrop	Baker
4/22/52	31 KT	Airdrop	Charlie
5/1/52	19 KT	Airdrop	Dog
5/7/52	12 KT	Tower	Easy
5/25/52	11 KT	Tower	Fox
6/1/52	15 KT	Tower	George
6/5/52	14 KT	Tower	How

vi. This report (co-published with Don Hibbard) led to a treasured career achievement. Based on the quality and new geological knowledge contained in the Nevada Test Site report, my colleagues in the Geological Society of America (GSA) nominated me as a GSA Fellow. I had joined GSA years before because some of its publications are relevant to the oil and gas industry, which is why I maintain my membership to this day. Nearly all of its membership is comprised of college professors, research scientists and USGS personnel, but very few petroleum geologists. Fellows are recognized for their many years of research, for publications and for extended service to the Society.

vii. Elastic waves are generated by exploding small, buried dynamite charges–or only by the vibration caused by the movement of large trucks or even by dropping heavy weights on the ground. The energy charges (shotpoints) are laid out in a straight line up to twenty miles long and a few hundred to several hundred feet apart. The transmission speed of the elastic wave varies with the medium it travels through. The velocity of sound in air is 1086 feet per second, with correction for temperature and barometric pressure. In water, velocity is several times faster, about 5000 feet per second. In rock, the sound velocity is even faster–up to 20,000 feet per second, depending on the rock

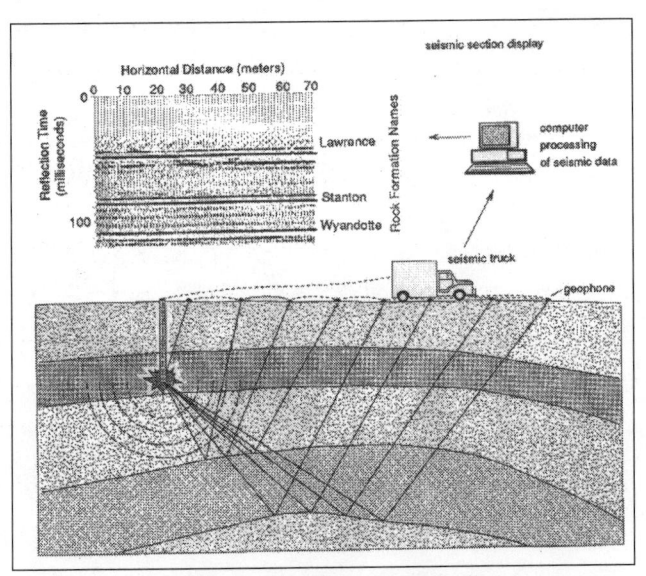

Figure 4. A schematic of how seismic data is produced, recorded, and displayed.

NOTES

type. Amazingly, seismic methods can record travel times in rock accurately to one-hundredth of one second.

The seismic echoes are detected by sensitive listening devices called geophones. These geophones are so sensitive that they can detect the shaking of the earth from a person walking past them. These geophones are placed in the relative proximity of the elastic-wave sources. The electronic recordings from these geophones are recorded on electronic devices for later retrieval. (Source: Walter Johnson)

The small dynamite charge and the raypath of the elastic energy are reflected to the surface to be detected by geophones, and are recorded with electronic instruments mounted in a truck (known as a "dog house"). The upper left side of figure 4 displays what the final seismic output would look like if the subsurface rock layers were horizontal. The seismic data looks like a cut through a layer cake, with the harder layers reflecting the most energy. (Courtesy of Walter Johnson)

Some rocks behave like sponges. A sponge placed on a liquid soaks up the liquid primarily from capillary action. In nature, oil and natural gas will move up vertically through rocks until stopped by reaching the apex of an anticline,

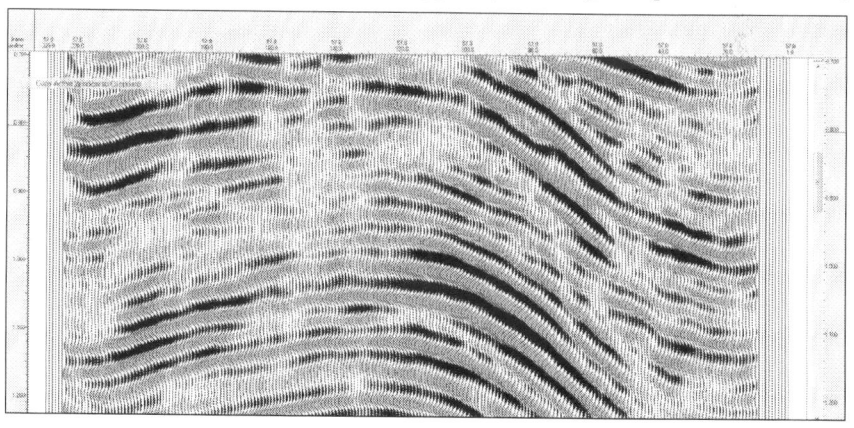

Figure 5. Seismic data over an anticline (data courtesy of U.S. Dept. of Energy).

which is an oil trap. The lower half of figure 4 and figure 5 show seismic reflections that depict a "sponge type" rock between two hard seismic reflectors revealing an anticline. In the earlier years of oil exploration, companies primarily explored for anticlines. Over time, more sophisticated geologic models were targets of oil and gas exploration. One such example is a reef type of objective. Figure 6 is a seismic section depicting an algal reef. Seismic data does not image the reef directly, but the impact of the vertical pinnacle of the reef can be seen on the surrounding rock, deposited after the reef. Figure 6 shows geologic events as wavy horizontal lines. The reef event (depicted by the second solid line from the top) protrudes through other geologic events.

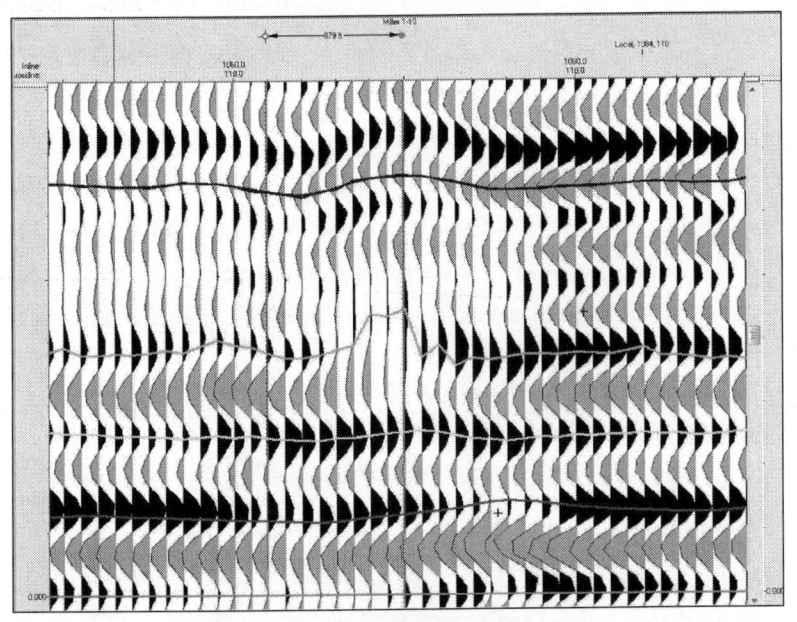

Figure 6. Seismic section over a reef
(data courtesy of Miller Energy).

viii. Thrust belts are layers of rocks, thousands of feet thick, that are folded and faulted (bent and broken) into complex assemblages that defy accurate geologic interpretation. In more technical terms, thrust belts are a series of mountainous foothills which form due to compression. Fold and thrust belts commonly form in continental forelands or basin margins due to the collision of tectonic plates.

ix. Raymond Plank, *A Small Difference* (New York: Vantage Press, 2012), pp. 115-119.

x. An override, or overriding royalty interest, is an interest in oil and gas production free and clear of all burdens and costs except taxes. It is commonly attached to assignments of oil and gas leases and contracts.

xi. A formation is a body of rock strata consisting dominantly of a certain lithology or lithologies or possessing other lithological features, up to thousands of feet thick and is the formal unit for subdividing the stratigraphic columns of an area. (Adapted from *Glossary of Geology*, Second Edition, Robert L. Bates and Julia A. Jackson, eds. Falls Church, Virginia: American Geological Institute, 1980, p. 242.)

xii. A section (geological section or stratigraphic section) is any sequence of rock units found in a given region either at the surface or subsurface. (Adapted from *Glossary of Geology*, Second Edition, Robert L. Bates and Julia A. Jackson, eds. Falls Church, Virginia: American Geological Institute, 1980, p. 258.)

xiii. The Athabasca oil sands consist of a mixture of crude bitumen, silica sand, clay minerals, and water. Some sands are exposed on the surface and are suitable for large-scale mining operations but most will be developed using in-situ technology.

Although the Athabasca tar sands were discovered in the 1700s, production did not begin until 1967 and was sporadic, due to Athabasca's inaccessibility and high recovery costs at variable and unattractive oil prices. However, production has recently surged because of demand and modern recovery technology. A government economic analysis several years ago estimated that 175 billion barrels of crude bitumen was economically recoverable, based on the West Texas Intermediate (WTI) crude oil benchmark price of 62 dollars per barrel. Recent major price variations require that these oil reserve estimates be lowered. Only 3% of the oil reserves have been recovered to date.

About 20% of the bitumen, about 35 billion barrels, will be recovered by open-pit mining using huge shovels capable of lifting tons of rock per scoop. The remaining 80%, comprising about 140 billion barrels, will be recovered using in-situ methods. This process requires a great deal of energy, which is being generated by the burning of natural gas supplied by Alberta's huge gas fields.

The town of Fort McMurray serves as the administrative center for Athabasca and two other major oil sand deposits, Peace River and Cold Lake. The combined owners and operators include Syncrude Canada Ltd., Suncor Energy and Albion Sands (owned by Shell, Chevron and Marathon). Husky, BP, and Conoco-Phillips also have interests in the area, as do some sixty other companies; these include one controlled by China that is proposing a pipeline to a Pacific coast terminal. All these operations have created an enormous mining, processing, and refining complex together with related services, employing up to 100,000 people.

In the mining operations at Athabasca, the overburden consists of up to 75 feet of muskeg, barren sand, and clay. The oil sands are 130 to 200 feet thick and are mined by huge tractor-driven shovels, standing three stories high. The sand deposit is crushed to loosen the sand grains, and hot water is added to form a slurry. It is transported to a huge vat-like container where the bitumen is recovered by flotation as froth. The bitumen is then separated from the solids and water and moved downstream for upgrading processing. After extraction, the sand is returned to the mined area and reclaimed.

The in-situ method used to process the Athabasca, Peace River and Cold Lake deposits is a steam-assisted, gravity-drainage, and cyclic-steam-stimulation system. Steam is injected through injection wells that heat the oil sands and reduce their viscosity. Based on a gravity-drainage principle, the heated bitumen sinks downward and is pumped to the surface by other vertically-drilled surface wells. Several pipelines transport the oil eastward and southward to Canadian and U.S. markets. The now-famous Keystone XL Pipeline that was scheduled to be built from Athabasca to U.S. Gulf Coast refineries is currently on hold due to political and environmental concerns.

xiv. For years, the oil industry attempted to develop economically viable techniques to artificially heat these oil shales to the required temperature of several hundred degrees and thus speed up the conversion process from millions of years to days. Currently there is little to no production from these shales, primarily due to the high temperature-conversion-process cost and environmental regulations imposed on the federal lands. However, the potential of oil shale reserves is huge.

xv. Hydraulic fracturing or "fracking" is a method of enhancing oil and gas recovery from wells by injecting water, sand and small amounts of chemicals into rock formations under very high pressure, to fracture the rock and release trapped hydrocarbons. It has been used in the industry for decades, but recent questions have arisen concerning possible environmental problems associated with fracking—especially suspected contamination of potable ground water, rivers and streams. Currently, the practice is regulated by the states and rules vary from state to state. However, some observers are asking for increased federal regulation to govern its use.

Over the years, significant advances have been made in materials and techniques, fracture modeling, fracture fluids and types of equipment needed. Today, over 60% of all oil and gas wells drilled worldwide are fracked. Many oil and gas fields would not be commercially productive without fracking. This includes Parshall. Coupling fracking with horizontal drilling has been instrumental in turning previously uneconomical and unconventional plays such as shale, shale oil, gas, and tight sand reservoirs into highly productive projects (as reported in a Kansas Geological Survey circular).

xvi. The U.S. is the only country in the world (except for parts of Canada) where the mineral wealth of the lands is shared by the federal government, the states, the Native Americans and private, non-governmental landowners.

In 1804, with the Louisiana Purchase, the U.S. acquired 828,000 square miles of land in mid America from France for only 15 million dollars. It almost doubled the size of the country. By various Acts and support of presidents, western migration of the people was encouraged. In the Homestead Act of 1862, settlers were granted 160 acres of public land conditioned by a requirement that they settle on it.

The passage of the Pacific Railroad Act, also in 1862, was the beginning of federal grants to railroads. In 1869, the first transcontinental railroad was completed between Council Bluffs, Iowa and San Francisco (1907 miles); then the U.S. government granted to the railroad alternate sections for ten miles on both sides of the track (a section is one square mile equaling 640 acres).

Various other actions of Congress ceded lands to Territories when they attained statehood and conveyed millions of acres to Native Americans for private reservations.

Mineral rights are separated from surface grazing and cultivation rights. Oil companies obtain the right to explore these lands through oil and gas leases negotiated with the mineral owners (using a standard oil and gas lease form adopted many years ago); such leases incorporate many rights retained by the mineral owner, including a royalty interest in any oil or gas that is found, produced and saved.

These unusual features of the American oil industry are vitally important because they allow the citizens, with their capital and entrepreneurship, the opportunity to discover and develop the oil and gas fields that are so beneficial to the economy and well-being of our country.

(Adapted from information generously provided by Robert J. Weimer, consulting geologist)

xvii. The atmosphere consists of four layers, totaling 62 miles high, which cover the earth and separate us from outer space. It is a mixture of nitrogen (78%), oxygen (21%), and other gases, a small percentage of which is carbon dioxide and other greenhouse gases such as methane and nitrous oxide. The sun's heat passes through the atmosphere to the earth, and the earth sends part of this heat back in a different form. It is the molecular structure of greenhouse gases (plus water vapor) that causes the trapping of part of this differently-reflected heat and prevents it from escaping into outer space. Burning fossil fuels generates more greenhouse gases, which in turn traps more heat, causing global warming. Additional sources of carbon emissions entering the atmosphere include the Mid-Atlantic Ridge and the world's animal waste. Deforestation destroys the sinks that absorb carbon. In the future, increased fossil-fuel use by the world's growing and thriving population (e.g., in India and China) will only compound the issue.

xviii. In November 1990, the Clean Air Amendments were signed into law by President George H.W. Bush. They provided for an emissions-trading system, which would allow utilities and companies exceeding their pollution quotas to trade their overages to another entity that is under its quota. This system became known as "cap and trade."

xix. Chlorofluorocarbons were used as refrigerator coolants and propellants for aerosol cans. It was believed that they were causing a hole to develop in the ozone layer in the Antarctic. Ozone beneficially absorbs ultraviolet radiation that causes skin cancer and protects plant and animal life.

xx. The Rio Accord, an international meeting called by the United Nations in Rio de Janeiro, was convened June 3-14, 1992 with the aim of reaching an agreement to limit greenhouse gases. The European nations wanted to establish specific timetables to reduce emissions and halt the destruction of natural resources and pollution of the planet. But some countries, including the United States, felt that there was too much uncertainty about the greenhouse gas issue and how it would affect each of their economies. Opposed were the developing and emerging countries such as China and India, which counted on burning coal (the cheapest energy source, but also the dirtiest) to grow their economies. Heads of state of 108 countries attended along with over 10,000 others, including scientists and observers. What came out of this mega-meeting was a plan to confine greenhouse gas emissions; its guidelines included adopting alternative energy resources to replace fossil fuels, creating new means of public transportation, raising awareness of the growing scarcity of water, and removing toxic components (like lead) in gasoline. Efforts to insure proper implementation would be reviewed in a future meeting in 1997.

xxi. The Kyoto Accord talks were held in Japan in December 1997 and attended by more than 12,000 officials, scientists, observers, industry representatives, and journalists. It committed parties to reducing greenhouse gas emissions, based on the premises that (a) global warming exists and (b) man-made CO_2 emissions have caused it. The U.S. refused to make the larger cuts in greenhouse gas emissions urged by the European Union. A settlement mandated binding CO_2 emission levels of 5% below 1990 emission levels, to be reached by the period of 2008 to 2012. This agreement excluded developing countries that opposed it. The U.S. signaled that it would not ratify any treaty that will commit it legally to reduce CO_2 emissions. The DOHA Amendment that would have committed the European nations to further reductions until 2020 was not ratified.

xxii. Very little was accomplished at the last three conferences. The very unproductive Copenhagen Climate Conference was held in December 2009. Talks were in disarray. To prevent a collapse of the summit meeting, a weak statement was adopted, drafted by the U.S., China, India and others. It recognized that climate change was one of the greatest challenges of the present day and proposed that action should be taken to keep climate temperature increases below two degrees Centigrade. It was not legally binding.

At the Warsaw Climate Conference in November 2013, with 195 nations attending, governments agreed to work on a universal climate agreement to be delivered at the Paris Conference in 2015. They also agreed to provide mechanisms to vulnerable nations so that they could better deal with extreme weather events. The agenda for the Paris Conference would include reducing deforestation and pollution from burning of fossil fuels.

The Lima, Peru talks, organized by the United Nations and concluded in November 2014, reached a compromise that was not fully supported. It would require all countries to submit plans to cut greenhouse gas emissions at the major Paris Conference to be held in December 2015. This departed from earlier agreements that put the emission burden only on the highly industrialized countries. A great deal of doubt existed that the poorer countries would comply.

xxiii. Dickinson Field is described in my 24-page RMAG publication appearing in *The Mountain Geologist* and titled "Dickinson Field Lodgepole Reservoir: Significance of This Waulsortian-Type Mound to Exploration in the Williston Basin," Vol. 32, No.3 (July 1995), pp. 55-79.

xxiv. Daniel M. Jarvie, Robert J. Coskey, Michael S. Johnson and Jay E. Leonard, "The Geology and Geochemistry of the Parshall Area, Mountrail County, North Dakota," chap. 9 in *The Bakken—Three Forks Petroleum System in the Williston Basin,* John W. Robinson, Julie A. LeFever, Stephanie B. Gaswirth, eds. Denver, Colo.: Rocky Mountain Association of Geologists, 2011, pp. 229-267.

xxv. Ten billion six-inch-long, one-hundred-dollar bills equal one trillion dollars, which converts to five billion feet. Five billion feet divided by 5280 feet equals 946,970 miles, which, divided by the circumference of the earth (24,901 miles), equals 38.03—the number of times that a string of one trillion dollars' worth of one-hundred-dollar bills would circle the earth.

ABOUT THE AUTHOR

Consulting petroleum geologist Michael S. Johnson is recognized for contributing to the landmark discovery of Parshall Field in North Dakota. His 68-year career in the Rocky Mountain region began with positions at Amerada Petroleum and Apache Oil. Since launching his independent consulting firm in 1963, he has focused his exploration efforts in the Williston Basin.

Born in 1926 in Missouri to Greek immigrant parents, he became increasingly intrigued with the oil business after his family moved in 1931 to Tulsa, Oklahoma, already the world's oil capital. He earned B.Sc. and M.S. degrees in geology from The Ohio State University.

His noteworthy and fulfilling career encompasses interests in several oil fields, culminating in his contribution to the discovery of North Dakota's Parshall Field. One of America's largest oil fields, Parshall extends over six million acres with producible reserves exceeding fifteen billion barrels.

Made in the USA
Coppell, TX
08 January 2020